A Jungian Approach to Spontar

In *A Jungian Approach to Spontaneous Drawing*, Patricia Anne Elwood provides an accessible and thought-provoking introduction to exploring spontaneous images, focusing on the value of this tool for insight into the unconscious. Illustrated with drawings of clients throughout, the book poignantly demonstrates how one can connect and access the spheres within through drawing, and how this process can reveal the unexpected.

Elwood begins by accessibly introducing key Jungian concepts and exploring Jung's belief in the power of spontaneity as an invaluable tool in one's journey to the soul. As well as illuminating spontaneity, an oft-forgotten aspect of Jung's psychology, she explores themes including structure and dynamics, symbols and archetypal patterns.

A Jungian Approach to Spontaneous Drawing also examines common motifs including houses, trees and people, and presents extended studies of work with children and adults and how their drawings relate and reveal Jungian ideas. Offering both practical and theoretical perspectives, this book demonstrates the universal benefits of spontaneous drawing for all age groups, helping people to find true release from unconscious blockages and traumas lying dormant in the depths of their own psyche.

A Jungian Approach to Spontaneous Drawing will be essential reading for Jungian analysts, Jungian psychotherapists and analytical psychologists in practice and in training, as well as art therapists with an interest in Jung, and those working with children and adults. It would also be of immense interest to students on courses including art psychotherapy, counselling psychology, Jungian psychology with art therapy, and all those in the helping professions.

Patricia Anne Elwood attended the Jung Institute in Zurich, where she completed her post-graduate diplomas in analytical psychology for children and adolescents and for adults. She lives and practices in Lausanne, Switzerland. She has taught in universities, as well as in clinical and educational fields and to professionals from a diversity of disciplines.

A Jungian Approach to Spontaneous Drawing

A Window on the Soul

Patricia Anne Elwood

Routledge
Taylor & Francis Group

LONDON AND NEW YORK

First published 2020
by Routledge
2 Park Square, Milton Park, Abingdon, Oxon OX14 4RN

and by Routledge
52 Vanderbilt Avenue, New York, NY 10017

Routledge is an imprint of the Taylor & Francis Group, an informa business

British Library Cataloguing-in-Publication Data
A catalogue record for this book is available from the British Library

Library of Congress Cataloging-in-Publication Data
Names: Elwood, Patricia Anne, author.
Title: A Jungian approach to spontaneous drawing : a window on the soul / Patricia Anne Elwood.
Description: Abingdon, Oxon ; New York, NY : Routledge, 2020.
Identifiers: LCCN 2019016496 (print) | LCCN 2019981101 (ebook) | ISBN 9780367209704 (paperback) | ISBN 9780367209698 (hardback) | ISBN 9780429264535 (ebook) | ISBN 9780429564024 (mobi) | ISBN 9780429559556 (epub) | ISBN 9780429555084 (pdf)
Subjects: LCSH: Jungian psychology. | Drawing. | Subconsciousness. | Psychology and art.
Classification: LCC BF173.J85 E49 2020 (print) | LCC BF173.J85 (ebook) | DDC 150.19/54—dc23
LC record available at https://lccn.loc.gov/2019016496
LC ebook record available at https://lccn.loc.gov/2019981101

ISBN: 978-0-367-20969-8 (hbk)
ISBN: 978-0-367-20970-4 (pbk)
ISBN: 978-0-429-26453-5 (ebk)

Typeset in Bembo
by Apex CoVantage, LLC

MIX
Paper from
responsible sources
FSC
www.fsc.org   FSC™ C013985

Printed in the United Kingdom
by Henry Ling Limited

Contents

Acknowledgements | vii

Preface | ix

Introduction | 1

1 Jung's journey to the soul | 7

2 Structure and dynamics in drawings | 13

3 Psychic energy or libido | 43

4 Janie and "The Wall" | 55

5 The symbol | 69

6 The collective unconscious: instincts and archetypes | 75

7 The transcendent function | 79

8 Alfonso and "The Red Toad" | 89

9 Totemism | 101

10 Bobby and "The Fish" | 109

11 The tree drawing | 129

12 The house drawing | 145

Contents

13   **The person drawing**   161

      What to observe in a drawing   181

      Conclusion   183

      Index   185

Acknowledgements

I am so very grateful to those who have participated in making this edition possible. First and foremost I thank Philippe Glatz, President of the Grangettes Foundation in Geneva, for stepping across a psychological threshold and joining me in my world of fantasy and perception. Without Philippe's curiosity, understanding, insight and support this edition would never have come to fruition.

I must also thank most sincerely Susan Tiberghien, the Jungian author and lecturer, who accompanied my process from novice to writer with faith and encouragement.

I remain sincerely grateful to the graphic artist, Enzo Messi of Messi Associates in Lausanne for his untiring support and input all throughout the process of production of this book.

I must mention all those in my practice and teaching groups who have supported my work and approach with unwavering confidence and who have permitted publication often of their most intimate drawings and personal stories.

Last but not least, I thank Janie, Bobby, Amy, Alfonso, Maddy, Martha and Billy and all those who entrusted their dreams and drawings and for the joy we have shared together in exploring what the psyche had to say about their lives and processes.

Preface

Jung relates his experience of drawing class when he was a child in his *Memories, Dreams and Reflections*:

> *My fear of failure and my sense of smallness in face of the vast world around me created in me not only a dislike but a kind of silent despair which completely ruined school for me. In addition I was exempted from drawing classes on grounds of utter incapacity. This in a way was welcome to me, since it gave me more free time; but on the other hand it was a fresh defeat, since I had some facility in drawing, although I did not realize that it depended essentially on the way I was feeling. I could draw only what stirred my imagination. But I was forced to copy prints of Greek gods with sightless eyes, and when that wouldn't go properly the teacher obviously thought I needed something more naturalistic and set before me the picture of a goat's head. This assignment I failed completely, and that was the end of my drawing classes.*[1]

When I was a child I used to draw trees with long, deep roots. I didn't know then that I was already seeking a deeper connection to the unconscious, that I was looking for the security one finds in that deep-rooted connectedness with the "Self" within.

Today, even after several decades of analysing, when I come back to my original instinct to draw I still draw trees with big roots, and I still feel a certain stabilising effect. My first recognition of the effect of spontaneous drawing has remained with me unchanged, intact, beyond time and events. I had discovered at an early age that drawing leads to that other place and space beyond the ego in a natural way.

Often when mothers or fathers are waiting in the waiting room for their children I ask them to draw something simple: for example, "*While you are waiting, draw me a tree.*" They have most often responded with pleasure at re-finding spontaneity in themselves, a space where they can let go and just "be" who they are in their own originality. They rediscover the deep-rooted joy in the most immediate and unexpected place, in front of a white sheet of paper with coloured crayons and pencils.

When Jung embarked on a deeper exploration into his own unconscious at 38 years old, he felt the need to return to the young creative boy in himself. He decided it was even necessary as a means of contacting his own spontaneous inner self. He pondered: "*The small boy is still around and possesses a creative life which I lack. But how can I make my way to it? I had no choice but to return to it and take up once more that child's life with his childish games. This was a turning point in my fate, but I gave in only after endless resistances and with a sense of recognition.*"[2]

Returning to meet the creative child archetype within, as Jung describes, can truly provoke a turning point. It is even a psychological fact that, very often in life, when all has been achieved or when the energy invested in a certain direction gets worn out, there emerges a desire to pick up the thread with some hitherto buried potential which had awakened in childhood but which got repressed in favour of other choices. The child, as an archetype, accompanies us all through life to the end. Unfortunately as adults we lose access to our spontaneous creative childishness; but presented with a blank sheet of paper and crayons, some instinct takes on life again, allowing a natural freedom that premeditation cannot produce.

My own passion for drawings was sustained, not by any personal artistic talents, but from the sheer awe in the limitlessness, the infinite variety, which I discovered through this medium. The drawing, like the unconscious itself, is something very close to us, and yet, like the unconscious itself, seldom recognised for what it truly reveals, seldom understood.

I discovered Carl Jung's ideas at 18 years old, when I was a student at Liverpool College at the end of the 1960s. Our curriculum included three semesters of Freudian psychology but one afternoon our psychology professor took time out to speak about Carl Jung and his collected works. The effect on my own psyche was immediate. The message had come like a revelation, an illumination: Jung had credibility for me that I had not hitherto experienced; it felt like an awakening. I remember feeling a sensation of tremendous relief in learning that someone called Carl Jung had understood what psyche and the depths are all about. I had found Freud inspiring and loved to read through his literary genius but Jung had opened a new door for me, a new dimension that has remained a source of reference throughout my life.

Several meaningful coincidences, which Jung has called "synchronicities," eventually led me to the Jung Institute in Zurich, where I took up my place on the benches and where I completed two post-graduate programmes, the first in analytical psychology for children and adolescents, the second in analytical psychology for adults.

From my beginnings in the Institute I was attracted to the magic of drawings, paintings and all art forms that provide channels for unconscious expression. I quickly perceived that spontaneous drawings contain some unconscious intention and that this may be revealed at any age, with any cultural background. As Jung himself through his works had opened a new door, here I found myself again peeping through another window.

Since I had no experience I was obliged to do what Jung professes: "*let things happen in the psyche.*"[3] As an observer, I realised that this other mind which was speaking through the drawings had an autonomy and direction of its own, which the conscious mind did not necessarily know anything about. However, once revealed, the observer, as well as the person drawing, can only admit the reality of the findings.

Over the decades I had read books on the interpretation of drawings and had so often felt unsatisfied; something was not quite right, like in a puzzle, where some fundamental piece is missing. As I could not attribute any real credibility to what I was reading I desired to seek further. Comparative studies were not sufficient: as with the psyche itself, I needed a greater understanding; I needed a map, a valid guideline, a means of apprehending the source and a comprehension of its dynamics.

As it became more and more obvious that on the hinterland of the drawing, another mind was activated from which the drawing found its source, I sought to discover more about this backyard of the psyche. Carl Jung had the key, and throughout the volumes of his collected works he made it accessible. This gradually became the level at which I was inspired to perceive and explore.

The hinterland of all authentic expression is the unconscious itself, and therefore in the spontaneous drawing there is inevitably a manifestation directly linked to the unconscious.

In my exploration and personnel understanding of the psyche as described and experienced by Carl Jung I found my key to the door. Since a first "Eureka," I discovered that the spontaneous drawing is a pure expression from the unconscious, and therefore its true comprehension is based on the deeper understanding of the structure and dynamics of the psyche itself.

From that day onwards I perceive the drawing as a window on the psyche, on the unconscious, one may even say, through the revelation of images from hitherto unknown realms, a window on the soul.

Patricia Anne Elwood

Notes

1 Jaffé, A. and Jung, C.G. *Memories, Dreams and Reflections*, Vintage Books, 1989, p. 29.
2 Ibid. p. 174.
3 Jung, C.G. *Collected Works* (abbrev. *CW*) Vol. 13, *Alchemical Studies*, Bollingen Series XX, Princeton University Press, 1967, p. 16, para. 20.

Introduction

This book is about the unconscious and how it expresses itself through the simple and most effective practice of spontaneous drawing.

The word "spontaneous" comes from its Latin root, "*sponte*," meaning "*of one's own accord, freely, willingly; acting voluntarily and from natural prompting; coming freely and without premeditation or effort.*"[1]

Spontaneous drawing has had but little recognition as a tool to accessing the deeper levels in oneself or in others. History reveals that this theme is hardly ever considered in the discipline of psychology and even less in psychiatry. If it is ever referred to, it usually only addresses children's drawings.

In fact spontaneous drawing from a Jungian perspective is not confined to any age group; it is universal and can be addressed to any person, of any age, sex, cultural background or religion, and goes far beyond childish expression.

Within the various schools of art at the beginning of the 20th century many artists, curious about the results produced through spontaneity, plunged daringly into a psychic "no man's land" with what were then modern modes of exploration.

The method of using spontaneous drawings as a tool for investigating the psyche acquired some importance with the development of child analysis in 1920s. Prior to this era there is no record of attributing any value even to children's drawings. From Palaeolithic times to the Renaissance we do not find any drawings by children and to such an extent that we wonder if children ever did indulge in this mode of expression. Palaeolithic cave paintings dating back as far as 35,000 years were obviously not spontaneous; they were stylised art forms which were invested with considerable preparation and most certainly even complex ritualistic procedures.

In the 1940s "Action Painting" introduced the value of the spontaneous artistic action and still holds its ground today. "Art Brut" or "Outsider Art" was established in the 1940s by Jean Dubuffet, a French artist who recognised this art form, but he considered it more within the spectrum of uncultivated, rather than spontaneous, art. What was important about Jean Dubuffet's enterprise for psychology was the fact that he took the art of the "outsiders" and the mentally ill seriously and investigated it with fervour. Jean Dubuffet was interested in the non-culture-bound drawings and art works of mostly anonymous characters. A famous collection is housed in the *Musée de l'Art Brut* in Lausanne, Switzerland.

Jung and his collaborators propagated the method of spontaneous drawing and spontaneous artistic expression as a real psychological tool for access to the unconscious and its processes. In the Jung Institute in Zurich the "Bildarchiv," or "Archive of Images," contains a huge collection of spontaneous art works dating from the time of Jung.

What Goethe's Faust claimed – "*Now let me dare to open wide the gate past which men's steps have never flinching trod,*"[2] – Jung accomplished. Opening those gates for Jung meant delving into the depths of his own unconscious, and his access was through spontaneity. Jung himself drew, painted and sculpted all his life. Every stage of his self-exploration was accompanied by the taking up of pen, pencil, brush or chisel, and plunging once again into this zone of unknowing so as to allow the unconscious to have its way through spontaneity. He admits he didn't always know where this would lead him, but he distinctly felt that despite a lack of rational understanding, he could follow the intuition that his drawings were highly significant. During the period in his life when he lost all outer orientation he turned inwards and began drawing mandalas daily.

Apart from Jung himself, who had persistently resorted to spontaneous activities as a means of creating a valid channel for the expressions coming directly from the unconscious, I have had two principal Jungian predecessors who have investigated the value of the spontaneous drawing as a precious indicator for somatic and psychic processes.

Susan Bach, born in Berlin in 1902, worked essentially with severely ill children and somatic situations. Susan had had a scientific background studying firstly crystallography but she gradually became more convinced of the irrational reality that spontaneous drawings offered.

In the 1930s as a refugee fleeing from the rise of Nazism in Germany she worked in mental hospitals in London, where she pioneered a movement introducing art as a therapeutic tool. She worked with children suffering from leukaemia and observed how the unconscious of the child perceived the illness through drawings. She soon discovered that the spontaneous drawing revealed suggestions for prognosis and diagnosis in illness.

Susan believed that spontaneous drawings accurately reflect somatic and psychological states. She followed the concepts of Jung at a time when the proof of the unconscious as a subconscious reality was being explored. Through her work she contributed to proving that the unconscious was indeed a source and a reality.

The basics of her work and research were published in 1990 in a book entitled *Life Paints Its Own Span: On the Significance of Spontaneous Pictures by Severely Ill Children.*[3] Susan died in London in 1995.

In 1985 I was walking towards the Institute in Zurich when I was joined by a fellow on the path who inquired about my studies. I was on my way to my propaedeutic exam and I had a collection of drawings in my folder. I told him what I was doing and that my exam was about the interpretation of images from the unconscious. He told me he was interested in that approach as well and asked to see the drawings I had in my bag. As I unfolded them he exclaimed that they were in fact the drawings he himself had collected throughout many years of inquiry into the unconscious. We were both surprised by the synchronicity of our timely meeting. His name was Gregg Furth and in 1988 he wrote a reference book in my field entitled *The Secret World of Drawings: A Jungian Approach to Healing through Art.*[4]

We met again a few times over the years and later in London in 2002; he confirmed that he was delighted that I had still retained the passion for the approach with drawings. Gregg had studied with Elisabeth Kübler-Ross and Susan Bach. He contributed to the works of Kübler-Ross on death and dying. Gregg passed away in 2005. I felt he had very generously passed onto me the mission to carry the exploration of spontaneous drawings further.

Originally I was inspired by the spontaneous drawing as a means of accessing the unconscious as its possibilities are limitless, it is easily organised, the material needed is minimal, it can be carried out anywhere, and is instinctively easy and attractive for most people.

This book is meant to illustrate, through some concrete material, that spontaneous drawing provides access to the psyche and can even produce processes that are unexpected for the conscious mind. It follows a Jungian approach and includes an introduction to the psychology of Jung.

This work attempts to encourage others to access their unconscious through this simple method. It is also meant to provide a tool for those working in the helping professions who need to refresh their therapeutic proposals, and as an alternative to a purely rational approach. The fact that spontaneous drawing is accessible to all beyond age, culture and religion, and often even beyond pathology, means that it may be applicable in many domains. One specific aim is to provide an authentic direction in analysis or diagnostic insight in certain pathological cases. It may be explored and tested in an endless variety of fields.

The analysis of spontaneous drawings is a science and an art. As a science one needs a basic understanding of the structure and dynamics of the psyche as well as experience with symbolism and unconscious processes. As an art it requires experience and encompasses all the functions of the psyche, feeling, thinking, sensation and intuition.

Jung says in his famous *Red Book,* which I prefer to call *Liber Novus,* as he himself entitled it: "*the wealth of the soul exists in images*,"[5] but he also goes on to say: "*scholarliness is not enough, there is knowledge of the heart that gives deeper insight*."[6] It is this knowledge of the heart that one must open to, so as to be able to grasp the mind in the background that is expressing itself through the drawing. This is an acquired art that goes with self-development and empirical experience. Letting go of the thinking mind to reach the level of the irrational pre-logical mind is what Jung had to do and which he advocates.

Jung prescribes:

I should advise you to put it all down as beautifully as you can — in some beautifully bound book. It will seem as if you were making the visions banal — but then you need to do that — then you are freed from the power of them. If you do that with these eyes for instance they will cease to draw you. You should never try to make the visions come again. Think of it in your imagination and try to paint it. Then when these things are in some precious book you can go to the book and turn over the pages and for you it will be your church, your cathedral — the silent places of your spirit where you will find renewal. If anyone tells you that it is morbid or neurotic and you listen to them — then you will lose your soul — for in that book is your soul.[7]

Notes

1   Extracts from *Oxford Dictionary of Etymology.*
2   von Goethe, J.W. *Faust in MDR's,* part II, p. 188–189 (vintage edition, 1989).
3   Susan, B. *Life Paints Its Own Span, on the Significance of Spontaneous Pictures for Severely Ill Children* (Daimon Verlag, Einsiedeln, 1990).

4   Furth, G. *The Secret World of Drawings: A Jungian Approach to Healing Through Art*. Published 2002 by Inner City Books (first published February 1989).

5   Jung, C.G. *The Red Book: Liber Novus (Liber Novus)*, edited by Sonu Shamdasani, translated by John Peck, Mark Kyburz and Sonu Shamdasani, W.W. Norton & Co, New York, 2009, p. 232.

6   Ibid. p. 233.

7   Ibid. p. 216.

Chapter One

Jung's journey to the soul

At the turn of the twentieth century, a new wave of exploration ran through Europe, creating an upheaval of the Victorian mind-set. The unconscious was gaining appreciation and many were interested in its discovery. Sigmund Freud had broken through the reigning taboos by overtly declaring his view on infantile sexuality and the unconscious. His book, "The Interpretation of Dreams," published in 1900, opened a door for many and heralded a new dimension in depth psychology.

Carl Jung, who was 19 years younger than Freud, had been treading a parallel path of initiation into the realms of the unconscious. Through dreams and visions he had been having since his early childhood he discovered that beyond the veil of the ego lay another mind, which had a personality all of its own and which expressed itself spontaneously.

This other mind which he observed in himself at a young age became a reality for him; he called it his "personality number 2." All his life Jung remained devoted to this "personality number 2," which expressed the language and intentions of the unconscious. He eventually referred to this inner voice in his famous *Red Book* as representing what he called "the spirit of the depths," which was opposed to a more conscious voice of "the spirit of the times."

Jung qualified in medicine in 1903, but eventually his passion and need to uncover the mystery of the psyche led him to take up a post in the Burgholzli mental hospital in Zurich. In 1903 psychiatry was not an enviable path to follow. Mental illness was treated with fear and even contempt, and few understood his choice when other more promising paths had been presented to him.

But psychiatry was also a domain that held many mysteries, and the mystery was provocation for Jung's curious mind. In Burgholzli Jung further witnessed this other mind speaking from the depths of the psyche in the mentally ill. He discovered themes and images which emerged spontaneously and which belonged to the memory bank of mankind that were not necessarily experienced in the patient's personal lifetime. He came to call this other layer beyond the personal sphere "the collective unconscious."

Once uncovered, this other layer further intrigued Jung. He had begun his career as a rational scientist testing and measuring reactions in the associations patients produced spontaneously to certain stimulus words. But gradually he became more convinced about what was for him at the time a more irrational approach to the unconscious.

In 1913, at the age of 38, Jung published his volume on *Symbols of Transformation*, which contradicted Freud's theories and created the break between them. He was by then a well-known psychiatrist on both sides of the Atlantic, a teaching professor in the Zurich University, with a privileged post in Burgholzli and a successful private practice.

Feeling the pressure of unanswered questions that had imposed themselves upon him, he decided he had come to an impasse in his development and research. He declared: "*The knowledge I was concerned with, or was seeking still, could not be found in the science of those days. I myself had to undergo the original experience, and, moreover, try to plant the results in the soil of reality.*"[1]

Jung had always had the intuition that the psyche has an ultimate aim and a final goal.

Reminiscing on his journey he declared:

No culture of the mind is enough to make a garden out of your soul. I had cultivated my spirit, the spirit of this time in me, but not that spirit of the depths that turns to the things of the soul, the world of the soul. The soul has its own peculiar world. Only the self enters in there, or the man who has completely become his self, he who is neither in events, nor in men, nor in his thoughts.[2]

To the surprise of many of his contemporaries Jung gave up his outer orientation in favour of a further exploration of the depths. He resigned from his post in the hospital and the university. He was seeking some final goal that he could not consciously define but which lay in the deeper layers of his own psyche on the level of the soul.

He felt that acts of spontaneous creativity would provide the access he was seeking to his own unconscious.

Jung had often taken steps that were other than his peers and contemporaries. His wife and ally, Emma, completely embraced his quest to understand the ultimate aim of the psyche. Emma was Jung's companion and friend who believed in his path and originally assisted him in his analytical research when he began his work with the association experiment.

In 1909 Jung met Toni Wolff, a young aristocrat with a vivid intelligence and a heightened psychological sensitivity. Her mother, following the death of her father, had referred Toni to Jung as a patient. Her bereavement was responsible for what was then termed as a "state of severe melancholy." Toni spent one year in analysis with Jung. One year after the ending of her analysis, their collaboration began. Toni, who had come through the depths of the darker zones in the psyche, was capable of holding the ground whilst Jung travelled through his own zones of obscurity.

As Jung began his self-inquiry, childhood memories surfaced which led the way back to spontaneous childhood activities he had once engaged in as a boy. He began collecting stones and pebbles by the lakeside and with them built little cottages, a castle, a village, as he had done in his childhood. At first he found this belittling, but eventually he was convinced that through these spontaneous building activities he was on the path to discovering his own myth. *"In the course of this activity my thoughts clarified, and I was able to grasp the fantasies whose presence in myself I dimly felt."*[3] *"For the building game was only a beginning, it released a stream of fantasies which I carefully wrote down."*[4]

Jung's personal journey, which lasted 14 years, was recorded in his famous *Red Book* which he entitled *Liber Novus*. He begins with an appeal: *"My soul where are you?,"*[5] a call that revealed the essence of his search. This calling seemed to have its origins in his adolescent days, when he felt frustrated at being denied any adequate responses to his questions about God and the mysteries.

In 1918–1919 Jung was on military service in Chateau d'Oex in the French-speaking part of Switzerland. It was there that he began spontaneously drawing mandalas daily. Gradually he came to see his mandalas as reflections of his inner state and eventually as the mirrors of the centre within himself. He says:

My mandalas were cryptograms concerning the state of the self which were presented to me anew each day. In them I saw the self— that is my whole being actively at work. To be sure, at first I could only dimly understand them: but they seemed to me highly significant and I guarded them like precious pearls. I had the distinct feeling that they were some-thing central, and in time I acquired through them a living conception of the self.[6]

Jung, in his own process of maturation, evolved from a rational thinker to an open-minded intuitive who became capable of apprehending deeper feelings without a need for understanding. He even welcomed the place of not knowing with curious enthusiasm. As regards the mandalas he had not fully realised the effect and what they eventually led to but he assiduously persisted in his drawings. Eventually though his dreams, drawings, his active imagination, his mandalas and his sponta-neous activities, he came to the centre in himself.

Jung was aware of the Hindu principal of "atman," which refers to the essence of pure being or pure conscience of being. The experience of atman includes the reali-sation of the purest form of "I am." Attaining an experience at the core gives insight into the aspect of self which is eternal, pure, undisturbed by and beyond emotions or preoccupations. Jung came to experience the equivalent of what the Hindus call "atman" through his mandalas. For him it was tantamount to perceiving the purest nature of the psyche itself and the most direct encounter with the Self within.

All through his personal research, spontaneity was the key channel for contacting the unconscious and Jung indulged in many approaches that encouraged spontaneous expression. Jung actually drew, painted and eventually sculpted in stone all his life. He was constantly seeking the connection to his own depths that spontaneity provides.

His methods produced a template for his patients, friends and collaborators. He encouraged those around him to follow a similar path towards the self through all forms of spontaneous imaginations, drawings and paintings. Many of his friends and contemporaries became passionate followers involved in what was then an exciting avant-garde movement. Jung's work and research provided a paradigm shift into an innovative approach where new ground was broken and hitherto mysterious dimen-sions were brought to light.

Jung attributed the greatest importance to the image itself. He believed that once emotions take form in images the conscious mind can actively participate in recy-cling the energies attached to the images, and subsequently return to a state of equi-librium. *"To the extent that I managed to translate the emotions into images – that is to say, find the images which were concealed in the emotions – I was inwardly calmed and reassured."*[7]

"The wealth of the soul exists in images."[8] This was Jung's personal credo.

Jung's intense introspection lasted 14 years until 1927. He says all his subsequent works found their source in this period of personal research. *"The years when I was pursuing my inner images were the most important in my life – in them everything essential was decided . . . It was the prima materia for a lifetime's work."⁹*

Even when Jung had found the ultimate image within, he knew the task he had set himself was not yet completed. He felt very strongly that he had to find parallels in history to validate his material and make his findings credible. He explored many fields: the philosophers, gnosis, ancient myths, Eastern religions. Eventually he found the link to the knowledge of the past in alchemy. He realised that the ancient alchemists of the past in their dark laboratories had followed a similar path to the Self which they described in symbolic language. He says, "*I had stumbled on the historical counterpart of my psychology of the unconscious. Only when I had familiarized myself with alchemy did I realize that the unconscious is a process and that the psyche is transformed or developed by the relationship of the ego to the contents of the unconscious.*"¹⁰

His exploration of alchemy and various alchemical texts heralded Jung's return to an active participation in the world.

As Jung's own process unfolded through his writings and his life history, his search for the soul became clear. The path he had taken to unveil the way to the ultimate goal of the psyche was revolutionary in his time. The fact that the psyche had a natural aim was an invitation into a spiral of mystery and discovery to which he remained devoted all his life.

For Jung, the soul is a universal entity and the way to the soul is through the longing to attain a centre at the core which is of the soul's own nature. Therefore for Jung, desire itself is of the soul: not desire geared towards any object, but that deep fundamental desire or nostalgic yearning to unite with the deeper layers within oneself. He says, "*If your creative force now turns to the place of the soul, you will see how your soul becomes green and how its field bears wonderful fruit.*"¹¹

But how did Jung mediate between what he discovered within himself and the belief systems of his time that had lost the sustaining matrix for the psychic disposition of modern man? These are profound questions that only an exploration of his works and life can answer.

Jung was a sage of our times. He turned back to the roots of knowledge as far as he could go and reaped a harvest of everlasting wisdom. He had always been known for his extraordinary erudition beginning in childhood with Hindu mythology, with Homer and Virgil, with Goethe's Faust and many others. Eventually going back to the mythological levels of man's own memory, he was versed in many facets of man's historical knowledge. But what was even more important was the fact that he had found the link that provided the continuum, through knowledge, of man's own psychic history.

Jung died in his home in Küsnacht on June 6, 1961, at the age of 86. All the questions he posed remain relevant in our modern times. The path he describes through his personal experiences remains accessible, the tools he used are also at our disposal and easily available: dialogue, creative expression through drawing and painting. He said: "*Our age is seeking a new spring of life. I found one and drank of it and the water tasted good.*"[12]

Notes

1 Jaffé and Jung, *Memories*, p. 192.
2 Jung, *Liber Novus*, p. 142.
3 Jaffé and Jung, *Memories*, Ibid. p. 174.
4 Ibid. p. 175.
5 Jung, *Liber Novus*, p. 232.
6 Jaffé and Jung, *Memories*, p. 196.
7 Ibid. p. 177.
8 Jung, *Liber Novus*, p. 232.
9 Jaffé and Jung, *Memories*, p. 199.
10 Ibid. p. 209.
11 Jung, *Liber Novus*, p. 236.
12 Ibid. p. 210.

Chapter Two

Structure and dynamics in drawings

Since childhood Jung had always had an exceptional perception of the psyche in himself. He had already at a young age experienced unexpected dimensions through dreams, synchronicities and inner events. He eventually came to the conclusion that the psyche had much more to it than the modern mind-set recognised. Eventually he declared:

> *The psyche is the greatest of all cosmic wonders and the sine qua non of the world as an object. It is in the highest degree odd that Western man, with but very few – and even fewer – exceptions, apparently pays so little regard to this fact. Swamped by the knowledge of external objects, the subject of all knowledge has been temporarily eclipsed to the point of seeming non existence.*[1]

Through his personal research and observing himself and others objectively, he came to discover that the psyche does actually have a comprehensible dimension. As the body has an anatomy and a physiology, Jung found that the psyche has its own equivalent, which he defined as "the structure and dynamics." According to Jung, the structure of the psyche lies in its conscious and unconscious spheres. The dynamics of the psyche is determined by the flow of psychic energy underlying all psychic phenomena, which he termed "libido."

The conscious part, which is equated with the tip of the iceberg, contains the ego with its functions and attitudes. The unconscious has a personal layer and an impersonal layer with access to an even deeper sphere he called "psychoid." The latter is beyond images but the energies coming from this level eventually take on form in the higher spheres approaching consciousness.

Underlying all this, the psychic energy has a specific pattern or flow which Jung called "the progression and regression of libido." Jung discovered the structure and dynamics of the psyche in his own journey through the unconsciousness and confirmed his findings over many decades of analysis with others.

Structure

Structure refers to:

- the ego with its attitudes and functions
- the personal unconscious
- the impersonal or collective unconscious
- the psychoid spheres

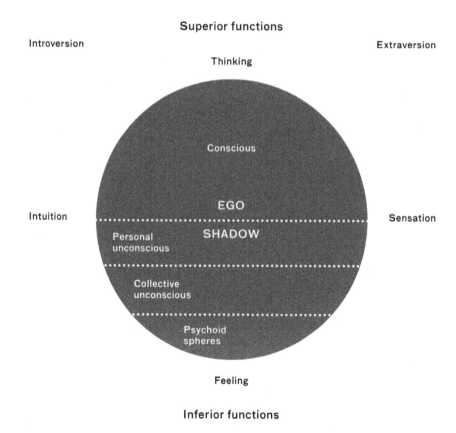

Attitudes

The ego has two fundamental attitudes common to all which Jung termed extraversion and introversion. As natural dispositions these are innate but not inherited. Every personality has both attitudes but there is always a preference, which is determined by the way in which the personality resources itself and builds up its energies. An extraverted personality needs contact with people and the outer world; the introvert, however, needs essentially to find his resources within himself.

The Functions

In the conscious field we find the ego with its natural modes of expression, which Jung called the functions. These are:

- thinking, a rational function
- feeling, a rational function
- intuition, an irrational function
- sensation, an irrational function (a function which corresponds to the capacity to organise details).

Every personality has a dominant function; thinking, feeling, intuition or sensation, which corresponds to what Jung called the "superior function." It is also the function through which the ego develops and expresses itself most easily and naturally. Through this function the ego deals with situations in the first half of life. In mid-life an intra-psychic change occurs and the accent on the superior function diminishes as other functions take on more importance. This is referred to as the mid-life shift.

The unconscious also contains a dominant function, which Jung refers to as the "inferior function," as it is not easily accessible to the ego and consciousness. It becomes more apparent in dreams, but in the mid-life shift there is a displacement, driven by instinct, where the ego tends towards developing its inferior function. A thinking type, for example, may suddenly seek out more meaningful channels for expressing a hitherto neglected feeling tendency. Or someone may want to take up some intellectual research tending towards a more thinking function after years of mothering or caring for others.

Feeling tone

Before any attempt at analysing a drawing we must first consider what Jung referred to as the "feeling tone" of the image. In approaching a drawing with focus and attention there occurs what Jung called an "*abaissement du niveau mental.*" This is a term he used to describe a lowering of psychic energy, which occurs when one pays specific attention to a motif or image. In this lowering of attention one may capture the atmosphere or "feeling tone" of a drawing and the impact it has upon us. It requires tuning into the drawing so as to be fully receptive to what is presented by the unconscious of the person drawing.

Introverted and extraverted attitudes are easily detected.

A typical extraverted attitude in a drawing.

An introverted attitude.

The personal unconscious

The personal unconscious contains all the personal experiences of the individual's life. It also contains all that has been learnt and acquired through growth and development. It stocks subliminal perceptions, and harbours emerging themes which are tending towards consciousness.

The collective unconscious

The collective unconscious, on the other hand, contains non-personal memories and may be called "the memory bank of humanity." It is the realm of instincts and archetypes. The images met at this level pertain more to mythological themes such as those we find in fairy tales and myths. This may also be called "the mythic level of the psyche."

A drawing may depict either a personal theme or a mythological theme. Personal themes in drawings indicate what is stocked in the personal unconscious based on primary experience, as well as on what has been learnt during the person's lifetime. Mythological themes, however, point to the fact that the energy in the psyche is moving at a deeper level where psyche produces themes and symbols out of itself.

In the interpretation of drawings firstly we perceive the structure, which involves where the motifs are placed on the drawing. Secondly we observe the underlying energy, determining its dynamics.

The structure in drawings is found in the position of the motifs.

Drawing on a vertical plane expresses a statement.

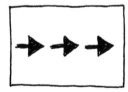

Drawing on a horizontal plane reveals a movement of psychic energy within a process.

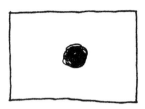

The ego lies in the centre.

The central position

The central position may correspond to a complex, or that which preoccupies the ego at the time of drawing. Complexes are what Jung defines as nuclei of energy accumulated in the unconscious that interfere with conscious intention. He says: *"they are psychic fragments which have been split off owing to traumatic influences or certain incompatible tendencies."*[2]

Drawing of an eight-year-old child who takes up a central position. Her comment: *"Someone pushed me and ran away, then my mum came to help."*

The ego lies in the centre.

Focus

Where does the main focus in the drawing lie? Is there one major point of focus or are there several?

This is the drawing of a 12-year-old who draws a battlefield with a tree and a pair of hearts.

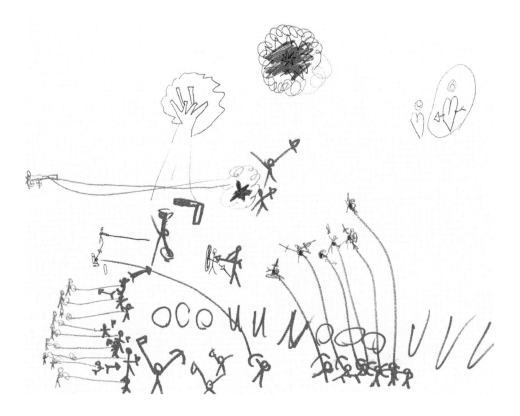

Coherence/incoherence

What is odd or incoherent with the rest of the drawing? What is incoherent or odd in the drawing arises out of the non-rational, pre-logical level of the psyche and therefore corresponds to unconscious elements being expressed.

What does the tree with broken branches have to do with the battle scene? And what do the two hearts refer to, the feeling function and its emotional states?

A series of drawings reveals a process in the psyche of the person.

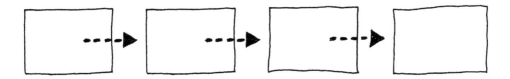

Auto-regulating function

According to Jung the psyche has an auto-regulating function. As the organs in the body seek to establish coordination and rebalancing so psychic energy tends towards harmony and equilibrium. This auto-regulating function becomes evident in a series of drawings where the unconscious unveils an underlying process and tends towards a psychic goal or the resolution of a situation.

Direction, movement, flow

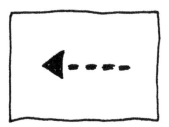

The direction the energy takes indicates where the orientation lies, tending towards the unconscious and regression, or towards progression, development and adaptation to the outer world.

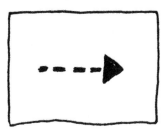

As we may have tendencies towards the right or left side of the drawing, we may also find tendencies towards the upper or lower spheres.

Upper spheres

With a tendency towards the upper spheres the positive aspect refers to everything that goes up, such as hopes, aspirations, ambitions, as well as joy and happiness. The negative aspect may be the mind level, preoccupations, feelings of weight and heaviness, overload.

Lower spheres

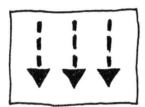

Point to a lowering of psychic energy, tending towards underlying motifs in the unconscious. This may correspond to a normal phase of regression, or to a more severe state of depression when energy is no longer available for activities in the outer world.

Centring

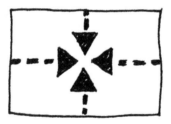

Movement towards the centre corresponds to what Jung called "centring." The movement towards the centre is positive and shows a tendency towards healing. Jung says; "*The centring process is, in my experience, the never-to-be-surpassed climax of the whole development, and is characterized as such by the fact that it brings with it the greatest possible therapeutic effect.*"[3]

Numbers

Numbers and repetition of numbers indicate that some element in the unconscious is seeking attention and needs to be integrated into consciousness. Numbers often point to dates or ages at which events or traumas took place.

Here there are eight apples in the tree and a ninth on the ground. At nine years old, the broken off branch represents the time when parents separated, a time of rupture and major loss for this child.

When the spontaneous drawing reveals some preoccupation on the part of the unconscious, the aim is to acquire a conscious participation in what is revealed, or as Jung says, "constellated." This conscious attention activates a dynamic process in which the unconscious responds to the ego attitude. We may refer to this as the ego/unconscious dialogue.

Repetitions in drawings

Repetitions often reveal that some underlying complex is activated; some unresolved issue from the past is still gathering energy in the unconscious.

Splits, divisions and broken-off pieces

These may point to ruptures in development or in the direction life takes. They may indicate losses or separations, divorces, moves, etc.

A tree of a 55-year-old man is split in three (see next page). There is also a repetition of the number three in his drawing, three branches on the upper right-hand side, three fir trees, and three branches to the smaller tree on the lower right. Once questioned he easily recognises his third attempt to build his life in a new environment.

Knots, holes, broken-off branches

These refer to significant moments in development when some marked events occurred.

If we take the tree as representing the tree of the life of the person then we may measure the years according to the height of the tree. The knot here is not quite half way up the tree.

Tim is six years old, what could be the significant event which occurred when he was two-and-a-half to three years old?

The tree of another six-year-old where the unconscious registers an event at about four years old.

Sometimes it is the birth of another child, as in the drawing of Tammy at five years old whose sister was born when she was three.

Missing motifs

Susie at 14 years old draws her family. The missing hands indicate her lack of means to find her place in the family but also her feeling of impotence in finding her sense of identity and place in the world.

Framing

Frames may be protective or emphatic. Framing an image, making it more outstanding, underlines its importance for the subject. Frames, like windows may invite inside as when looking from the outside in, or they may represent an inner sphere from which one looks outwards.

Barriers

Barriers may refer to containment, a holding within. They represent protection, privacy or a need for intimacy as in family secrets where certain truths must not be exposed. But they may also symbolise rejection, introversion or isolation, being cut off from the outside world and others.

There is a family secret here, four inhabitants have now become three, but no one wants this to be known outside of the family circle.

Off the page

Shows a lack of involvement, fear of commitment and a shying away from the task reflecting a basic lack of confidence and sense of self.

Cut-off image

Indicates a rupture in the progressive development, an interruption in the process of growth or a radical change in direction in life.

The ego

Jung defines the ego as: "*A complex of ideas, which constitutes the centre of our field of consciousness and appears to possess a high degree of continuity and identity.*"[4] One may say the ego is the organ of our conscious identity. It develops from its own matrix, the unconscious, and separates out from the unconscious through the development of the sense organs. The ego develops in the first half of life through its functions and attains a sense of self or a sense of its own uniqueness. In delving into the psyche one must also pay attention to the state of the ego.

In spontaneous drawings the ego may find a central position or be dual, as in symbiosis or identification, or it may also be dispersed or fragmented as in severely neurotic or psychotic cases.

An ego becomes weakened when there is severe repression, or when the flow of libido has been blocked over a certain length of time. In this state the ego may become inundated with incompatible contents coming from the unconscious that are too powerful for integration. An ego which is overwhelmed with archetypal or impersonal themes coming from a highly charged unconscious may well show signs of its fragmented state in a spontaneous drawing. In the case of unwelcome intrusion of repressed contents from the unconscious the auto-regulating function of the ego may be lost and psychological themes take on an archaic form.

The invasion of psychic contents coming from the deeper repressed levels may lead to inundation of the ego and what we call neurosis or even psychosis. The unconscious regulation is necessary for mental and physical health.

Dispersion

In lesser cases when there is splitting but where the ego is not completely over-whelmed, as in neurotic structures, there may be dispersion and lack of association amongst the motifs. With dispersion, there is a lack of cohesion, of centring, and of a specific theme.

Fragmentation

When the ego is inundated we get a pattern of fragmentation.

The drawing of "a person" from a child of eight whose ego is in a state of inundation . . .

... and his "giant."

Identification

The ego may also be in a state of identification, as with peers, or in a symbiotic relationship.

"My Best Friends."

Jimmy is identified with his dad.

The ego in a centred position shows that the sense of self is acquired and even well established.

"Here I am!"

The ego is not equated with the whole of the psyche; it is the organ which channels consciousness but it is not the greater part of the whole: *"The ego as a complex does not comprise the total human being; it has forgotten infinitely more than it knows. It has heard and seen an infinite amount of which it has never become conscious. There are thoughts that spring up beyond the range of consciousness, fully formed and complete, and it knows nothing of them."*[5]

Some of these thoughts, stocked in the unconscious, tend towards consciousness, and may even impose themselves as they have an intention of their own and seek to be recognised. They may appear unexpectedly in spontaneous drawings.

Notes

1   Jung, C.G. *CW* Vol. 8, Routledge & Kegan Paul, 1960, p. 169.
2   Jaffé and Jung, *Memories*, p. 393.
3   Jung, C.G. *CW* Vol. 8, p. 203, para. 401.
4   Jung, C.G. *CW* Vol. 6, Bollingen Series, Princeton University Press, 1971, p. 425, para. 706.
5   Jung, C.G. *CW* Vol. 8, p. 324, para. 613.

Chapter Three

Psychic energy or libido

As blood flows in the physical body, psychic energy or "libido" flows in the psyche. We have seen that drawings have an underlying structure in the spatial orientation and in the way the motifs are placed in a drawing. There is also an underlying energy determined by a tendency of the motifs to follow a certain direction. This energy Jung called "libido."

Jung differed from Freud in that he described libido as referring to all psychic energy and not just sexual energy. He did not deny the power of the sexual drive, but he placed it amongst other drives, affirming that, at the basis, hunger, under certain circumstances, may be even more important than the sexual drive.

Psychic energy, or "libido," has a specific pattern: it progresses or regresses. Jung states: "*One of the most important energetic phenomena of psychic life is the progression and regression of libido.*"[1] He explains: "*Progression could be defined as the daily advance of the process of psychological adaptation.*"[2] Here he is referring to the ego's adaptation to the environment, the outside world and conscious life. Regression, on the other hand, refers to a "going in" or psychological adaptation to the inner world.

Progression, regression

The underlying energy or libido, which in a state of progression tends towards the right side of the drawing, is concerned with adaptation to the concrete outer world. The regressive flow towards the left, points to the inner world and the unconscious.

Progression.

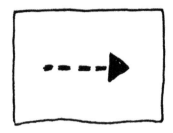

Regression.

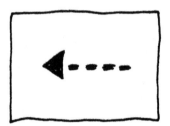

These directions of psychic energy in a drawing tell us if, at the time of drawing, there is an adaptation to the inner, or to the outer world.

Progression

Regression

Progression may not always be positive, as regression is not always negative. Successive progression may correspond to a flight forward and a refusal to turn towards any call to inner adaptation. Regression may belong to a retreat from outer confrontation and from adaptation to the environment. At every age and stage of development adaptation is called for according to inner and outer circumstances. Psychic energy must flow according to what Jung calls, "*Its own gradient: seeking its own goal.*" In regression the energy is redirected towards its matrix, the unconscious.

Here psychic energy refreshes itself before returning towards the concrete world and conscious life. This process occurs naturally at every age and stage of development and is especially noticeable at times of change in orientation or at times of readjustment when big decisions are being taken. When one meets a crossroads in life, it may happen that, as Jung says, "*A complete orientation towards the inner world becomes necessary until such a time as inner adaptation is attained. Once the adaptation is achieved, progression can begin again.*"[3]

Jung says: "*Man can meet the demands of outer necessity in an ideal way only if he is also adapted to his inner world, that is, if he is in harmony with himself. Conversely he can only adapt to his inner world and achieve harmony with himself when he is adapted to the environmental conditions.*"[4] By this we understand that inner adaptation is as important as adaptation to the outer world and its demands. Most people have experienced the need to go in at different times, to disconnect from the outer world and pay attention to inner feelings and moods. There comes a time to take time to walk in the forest, spend a day in the mountains, read a book or visit a church or temple.

Spontaneous drawing provides the perfect field for perceiving the direction and flow of libido and for just letting the unconscious express itself at will without interference or preconceived projection.

As in the life of a plant, where the source of the budding flower is in the roots, so psychological development proceeds out of the matrix of the unconscious.

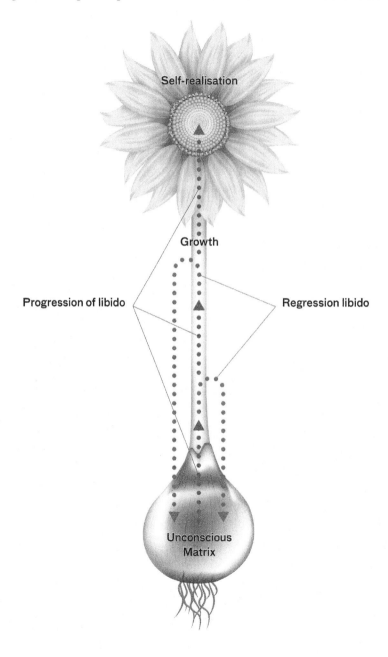

Jung never lost a sense of solidity within himself. Later in life reflecting on this he says:

> *Life has always seemed to me like a plant that lives on its rhizome. Its true life is invisible, hidden in the rhizome. The part that appears above ground lasts only a single summer. Then it withers away – an ephemeral apparition. When we think of the unending growth and decay of life and civilizations we cannot escape the impression of complete nullity. Yet I have never lost a sense of something that lives and endures underneath the eternal flux. What we see is the blossom which passes, the rhizome remains.*[5]

Libido patterns in myth

Many myths illustrate the patterns of progression and regression of libido. In myth, the hero must abandon the known world and regress, descend, or go beyond, towards the unknown spheres. Theseus, in the Greek legend, who descends into the labyrinth where he is obliged to embark on the journey towards the Minotaur, is a model of this pattern.

Theseus and the Minotaur by a 10-year-old girl.

Jonah in the belly of the whale also illustrates the movement of psychic energy. The descent of Jonah into the deep sea is symbolic of the regressing libido returning to its own base in the unconscious. Jonah journeying within the belly of the whale sees what Jung calls the "representations collectives," or visions. Finally, when the time comes, he finds himself returning to the shore of the world, renewed, even changed, and more able to assume the task that God had ordained for him that he had previously shunned. This journey of descent is referred to as "The Night Sea Journey."

In the belly of the whale by an 11-year-old boy.

The meaning of the journey is transformation and progression to another level of development with a new extension of consciousness. The process of journeying corresponds to an initiation.

Although our Western culture and modern mind-set has lost the sense of initiation and initiation rites, which are no longer consciously supported in our society, they have not disappeared, but have become introverted and live on, intact, on an inner plane. In the deeper levels of the unconscious, for transformation to take place there has to be a combat, a struggle with the power of the depths. It is a place where the ego can no longer deny its fears. Its challenge is to assume the trials of the journey and free itself. And of course the hero is never the same again. He is transformed by the experience.

The night sea journey in the depths of the monster corresponds to the deeper realms of the unconscious where one is no longer in the familiar personal spheres but has gone further into the unknown. Jung says, "*For us the psyche does not stop where the blackness begins but continues right into the unconscious.*"[6]

In fairy tales the hero or heroine goes underground to meet the witch, the devil or other devourer. The devourer takes the hero away from normal life and presents him with a challenge. By venturing into the unknown and living the inner journey one can evolve to a further stage, to a higher sphere. The unconscious provides an unlimited variety of motifs of this pattern.

In anthropological evidence the San people of South Africa illustrated the same themes many thousands of years ago. Their drawings on cave walls go back to the origins of man's first forms of expression. The San people were devoted to a mythological animal called "Rainmaker," who had to be caught and then sent down to the underworld to find the sources which could be influenced to make it rain.

Rainmaker journeyed through the underworld before emerging to the conscious world once again. The intention in this journeying was to influence at the source so as to provide change and fertility.

The re-emerging represents the progression of libido that follows the descent and the transition.

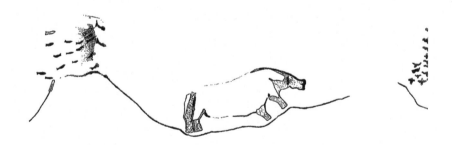

From ancient times man has told myths and stories to express the pattern of libido which is integral to his own psychic maturation, and his evolution. Although we may have but little conscious recognition of this process, these stages of regression, progression and initiation which live on in the unconscious are often clearly produced in a series of spontaneous drawings.

Blockage in the flow of libido

Just as the libido may be compared to a steady stream pouring its waters into the world of reality, so a resistance, dynamically considered, resembles, not a rock that juts up from the river bed and causes the stream to flow round it, but a flowing back towards the source. Part of the psyche really wants the external world object, but another part of it strives back to the subjective world, where the airy and lightly built palaces of fantasy beckon.[7]

The healthy progression and regression of libido can be blocked by a false attitude, by trauma, or lack of facilitation in the environment as when parental attitudes are contrary to a child's natural inclinations. Resistances to the natural flow of psychic energy from an inner or outer cause create blockages and with this stoppage energy gets damned up. This damned-up energy flowing back towards the unconscious stimulates inner images and fantasies.

When adaptation to the outer world is no longer possible because the flow of libido is blocked and has ceased to progress one finds that there is a lack of energy for the normal tasks of everyday life.

False attitudes and false adaptations belong to every age and stage of life. A child tending towards a new phase of development can refuse to advance desiring only to regress further into the mother. Or an inhibition may come from the outside, from a parent or teacher who does not recognise the innate potential of the child who therefore receives no mirroring and as a result becomes forced into a pattern of false adaptation.

Later in life there may be a refusal to let go of youth and the image of oneself as young, vital and capable. A defence develops against ageing, which inhibits the natural progression/regression of psychic energy and reinforces attachment to old worn-out patterns of behaviour. With this repetition of patterns that have no longer any meaning for the development of the personality, feelings of futility, worthlessness and depression may set in. In this case the normal flow has also been contradicted by a wrong attitude.

Jung believed that attitude was a very important factor and that attitudes are under our conscious control: "*We can satisfy the demands of adaptation only by means of a sufficiently directed attitude.*"[8] Attitudes can therefore be consciously influenced and readjusted.

In childhood there are several marked phases of progression and regression. Natural regression occurs when a new phase of development is being prepared. There is a going in before a new stage of going out. We often observe the phase of attachment to the mother and the inner world, followed by opposition and exploration of the environment, then once again a phase of return, before another phase of relative independence. During times of natural regression, when the attention to the outer world is lessened, there is not only a lack of energy for outer interests but there may also be a limited capacity for acquisitions. In this case, the approach is not to reinforce attempts to contradict the tendency but to recognise the state of the libido and work towards solving the situation of blockage. The persistent stagnation of psychic energy leads to neurosis and a halt in the process of maturation. When this occurs the therapeutic aim is to assist the psychic process until movement has taken over once again.

In this drawing, Philly, a five-year-old who would normally be extraverted and sociable, has her access to the outer world blocked.

Here we see she is on the verge of descent or regression as her drawing indicates.

And eventually there is a sinking into the lower spheres of the unconscious.

Before a resurgence of libido with a renewed sense of self.

Notes

1 Jung, C.G. *CW* Vol. 8, p. 32.
2 Ibid. p. 32.
3 Ibid. p. 36.
4 Ibid.
5 Jaffé and Jung, *Memories*, p. 4.
   5 Jung, C.G. *CW* Vol. 8, p. 39.
6 Jung, C.G. *CW* Vol. 5, Routledge & Kegan Paul, 1956, p. 173, para. 253.
7 Jung, C.G. *CW* Vol. 8, p. 16, para. 29.
8 Ibid. p. 32, para. 60.

Chapter Four

Janie and "The Wall"

When psychic energy regresses and the regression continues over a certain length of time, when progression is inhibited and no longer occurs, the ego finds itself in a state of powerlessness regarding its capacity to handle the demands of the outside world and the immediate environment. Former interests drop away, activities which were previously stimulating no longer hold any attraction, relating to others may become a source of stress or boredom. There may be a shying away from the world, a lack of energy for normal everyday tasks and even a difficulty in rising in the morning to face the day. Clinically this may be defined as a state of depression but Jung saw that this state of regression can actually be meaningful and that its aim is to lead to the possibility of discovering other unexpected dimensions within oneself.

This was how Janie felt when at 62 years old she came to a crossroads in her life and found herself in the depths of what she called her blackest night. Janie is unmarried and has no family members alive. She has recently been made redundant from her work and sees no future for herself, no meaning in life. Janie is a very introverted personality and often finds that through drawing she expresses herself better than with words.

This first drawing illustrates Janie's sensation of blockage and loneliness.

A next drawing Janie calls; "My Destiny."

In this state where there is a lack of energy for life Janie feels that her path has always been difficult, that to bear the burden has been her fate and that there is no possibility of change or hope for a better life. We note in her drawings that Janie also turns her back on life and has no connection to others. Everyday her depression seems to go deeper and becomes more and more oppressive.

Janie says the most alive part of her is her tears; in crying she can feel herself through the numbness.

Janie longs for the stars and other realms far away from the earth and suffering.

Janie calls the drawing on the facing page "The Nine holes of Hell" and claims that she knows all of them. Despite what Janie says we seem to observe some dynamic movement in the figures of her drawing which represent herself.

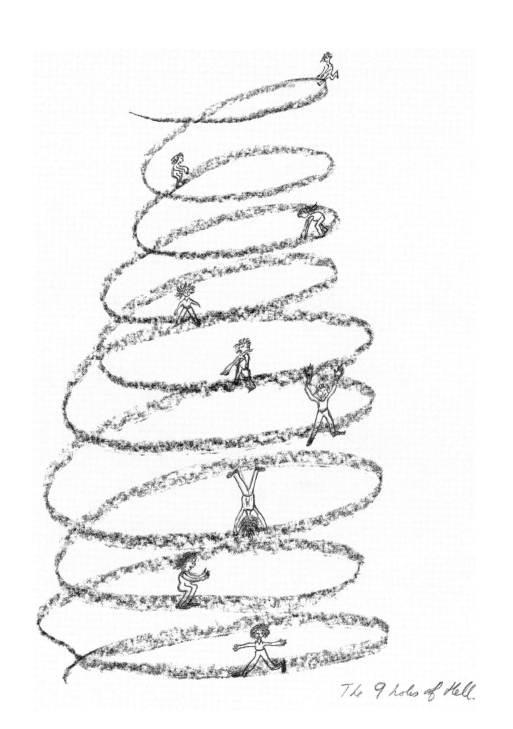

The 9 holes of Hell.

As the outer world is empty and void, the inner world takes on colour and meaning. Janie begins to take her inner world seriously and draws some of her dream figures she feels may be significant.

In one of her dreams Janie found herself on an island far away in a strange sea. As she continues her dream theme through active imagination she discovers that she is not alone on her island but is accompanied by two helpers. We also see that there is a vision of a new shore, a new earth.

Janie in her depression feels she was flung into outer space and has lost all contact with the earth and daily life. She realises that to surface again from the depths she must begin to ground so as to gather more energy.

She has the idea that she has to grow roots to be able to come back to earth and life as she knew it.

In another dream Janie meets "Green Man" a kind of earthy Pan figure who brings her a sensation of joy and solidity.

Green Man

She discovers that a kind of curiosity is awakening in her through her dream figures. She has more strength to connect with nature and the elements. In her everyday life, Janie is making contacts with new people. She even adopts an abandoned dog, which she calls "Dante"!

Little by little Janie develops a desire to rid herself of the sensations of weight and blockage. She relates this to pushing a black wall. With effort some new light can begin to pierce the darkness.

pushing the wall

Eventually in a dream Janie is visited by a red bird. She has found him in a back room in her house which she had forgotten and neglected for a very long time. She is surprised to find that he is still alive and well. She finds him very beautiful as if she is seeing him for the first time. She says he is so beautiful that no drawings could ever depict his loveliness.

Does this red bird refer to some deep buried potential in Janie herself that has been cut off and repressed from consciousness for some time?

Janie still feels she has a mountain to cross but as psychic energy moves once again into progression, her desire and curiosity for life begins to awaken, and she feels willing to attempt the climb.

There is a summit in sight!

And beyond the summit . . . a new sun is rising.

In the outer world Janie began to change her attitude and her way of relating. She begins to find pleasure in her newfound freedom as she can manage her days as she pleases.

Janie eventually decided to "reduce her persona," a phenomena which Jung describes, and which may occur later in life with an intra-psychic change. The attachment to the outer world and especially to the image one presents to the world becomes less accentuated in favour of a more meaningful inner connection to the self and the unconscious. In this phase one may feel guided as if the ego is no longer the determinant but something deeper is guiding the change. Janie who had an active professional career for many years has now let go of the image of herself as a successful and competent woman. She begins to take down some old books from her bookshelves and turns to an earlier interest she had in poetry and philosophy. Janie joins a poetry reading group where she is appreciated and receives a healthy mirroring in her newfound activity. She develops a new sense of well-being and begins to find contentment in her renewed sense of self. She comes to the conclusion that she now feels better than ever before and that she owes the change to her dark night journeying.

Janie is now retired and lives in peace with Dante in a small village on the outskirts of town. She says she is not afraid of dying but now, especially, not afraid of living either.

Dealing with the problems of life is not always obvious for the ego. Jung remarks:

> *Now and then it happened in my practice that a patient grew beyond himself because of unknown potentialities, and this became an experience of prime importance to me. In the meantime I had learned that all the greatest and most important problems of life are fundamentally insoluble. They must be so, for they express the necessary polarity inherent in every self-regulating system. They can never be solved but only outgrown. I therefore asked myself whether this outgrowing, this possibility of further psychic development, was not the normal thing, and whether getting stuck in conflict was pathological. Everyone must possess that higher level, at least in embryonic form, and must under favourable circumstances be able to develop this potentiality.[1]*

Note

1   Jung, *CW* Vol. 13, pp. 15, 18.

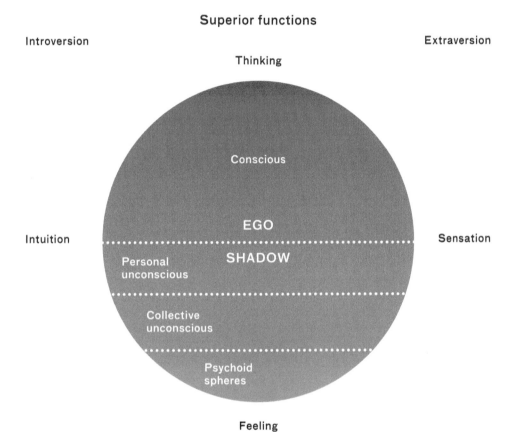

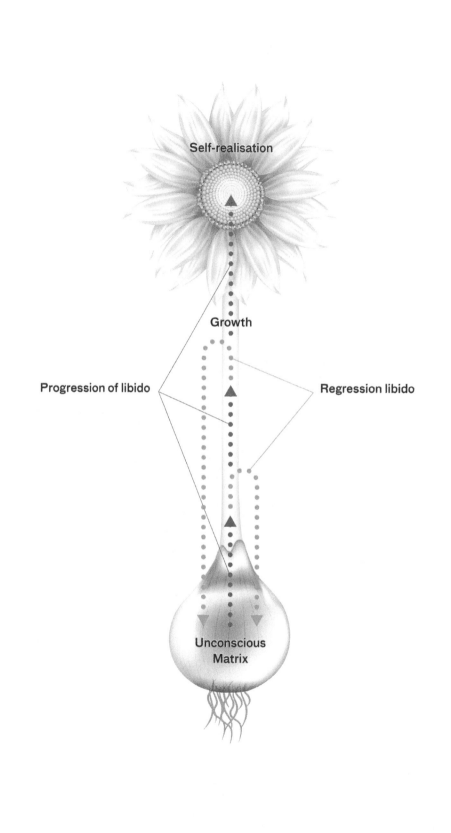

Self-realisation

Growth

Progression of libido

Regression libido

Unconscious
Matrix

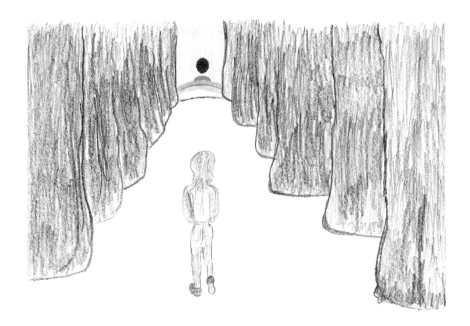

The 9 holes of Hell.

pushing the wall

Chapter Five

The symbol

The unconscious, as in dreams, speaks in images, which are symbols. Therefore the language of the psyche itself is symbolic language. All traditions communicate through symbolic language. Alchemy for example is rich in symbolism. The symbol communicates beyond the conscious mind and influences at a deep level.

Jung found that modern man does not take care of the symbolic language of life:

At a time when all available energy is spent in the investigation of nature, very little attention is paid to the essence of man, which is his psyche, although many researches are made into its conscious functions. But the really unknown part, which produces symbols, is still virtually unexplored. We receive signals from it every night, yet deciphering these communications seems to be such an odious task that very few people in the whole civilized world can be bothered with it. Man's greatest instrument, his psyche, is little thought of, if not actually mistrusted and despised. "It's only psychological" too often means: it is nothing.[1]

Jung had the highest regard for the power of symbols and their function in the psyche. He says: "*Considered from the standpoint of realism, the symbol is not of course an external truth, but it is psychologically true, for it was and is the bridge to all that is best in humanity.*"[2]

A symbol emerges from the deeper layers in the psyche and is therefore not something completely comprehensible as it always contains its own conscious and unconscious aspect. It is therefore apprehended, but not completely understood rationally.

How do we recognise a symbol from a sign? If one puts gas in the tank of a car, it is a straightforward description; therefore it is not a symbol. However, if one "puts a tiger" in the tank, this is symbolic. The tiger, in this context, suggests characteristics far beyond those possessed by gasoline, such as swiftness, power, even mystery.

"Symbols are not allegories and not signs: they are images of contents which for the most part transcend consciousness. We have still to discover that such contents are real, that they are agents with which it is not only possible but absolutely necessary for us to come to terms."[3]

We may consider any motif in a drawing as a symbol. When a symbol is produced we may focus on it, set it apart, isolate it or ask for it to be amplified. Approaching the symbol is primordial to the mobilisation of psychic energy. Symbols have a role to play which is of the utmost importance as activators in the process which carries and transforms psychic energy itself.

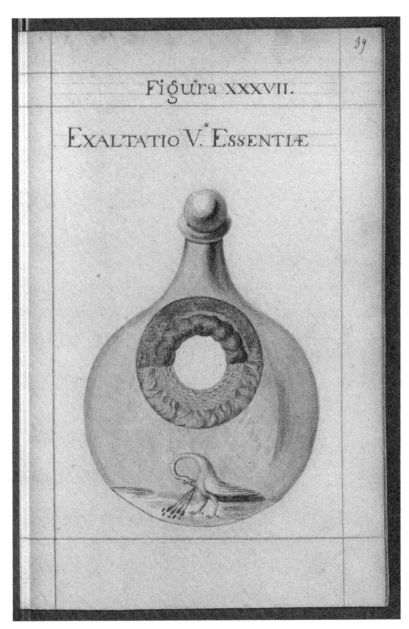

Source: Sapientia veterum philosophorum sive doctrina eorundem de summa et universali medicina.
18th c. Bibliothèque de l'Arsenal, Paris. Used with permission.

Sometimes a rising symbol is portrayed in the least obvious detail as it is still in the process of reaching consciousness and has not been given much conscious attention. Then it may be separated out and more closely investigated. Let me see what the owl in the tree is doing once he is taken out of the tree.

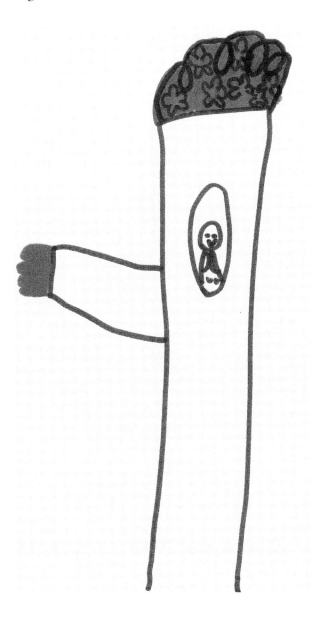

Symbols are natural attempts on the part of the psyche to unite the opposites; they are also personal and archetypal at the same time. Spontaneous drawings and dreams produce a personally composed symbolic language as well as collective themes. By paying attention to the symbol formation in the unconscious one participates in the symbolic life of the psyche.

Jung proposes there is a treasure to be unearthed in actively partaking in the symbolic dimension of life. He claims that without symbolism life is banal, superficial and ordinary. The stimulus provided by the symbols in our nightly journeying gets lost during the day, as the nocturnal images are not given any importance. "It is only a dream" is a common statement. There is no continuity as attention to inner images is lacking. To participate in the symbolic dimension of life one begins by taking the spontaneously produced symbols seriously. This may require some effort as symbols do not present themselves as rational entities; however, they do have a luring effect, and as one embarks on the journey of exploration the fascination leads ever onwards. Eventually a sense and feeling for the symbolic life develops, a consciousness of two dimensions corresponding and relating within one's own psyche. A dialogue begins; the unconscious responds.

Symbol formation is natural and represents what is enduring and common to all of mankind, beyond race, culture and even beyond evolution. Symbolic images bring the obscure regions of the psyche to light. They carry with them an alluring energy and a power to enchant.

Notes

1 Jung, *CW* Vol. 18, pp. 263, 606.
2 Jung, *CW* Vol. 5, p. 231, para. 343.
3 Ibid. p. 77, para. 114.

Chapter Six

The collective unconscious: instincts and archetypes

Jung informs us that the collective unconscious, corresponding to a deeper layer in the psyche beyond the personal unconscious, is identical in everyone. It is the realm of the universal memory bank of mankind. Within it there are themes, patterns and symbols which are accumulated through man's evolutionary history and which are common to all peoples. These collective themes, which find their expression in myths, unite us all on a universal plane.

Myths are archetypal, meaning that they demonstrate themes and characteristics which are common in any culture. Myths attract, fascinate and mobilise energy at a deep level. They also unconsciously set behaviour patterns into motion.

Speaking of the collective unconscious Jung says:

In addition to our immediate consciousness, which is of a thoroughly personal nature and which we believe to be the only empirical psyche (even if we tack on the personal unconscious as an appendix), there exists a second psychic system of a collective, universal, and impersonal nature which is identical in all individuals. This collective unconscious does not develop individually but is inherited. It consists of pre-existent forms, the archetypes, which can only become conscious secondarily and which give definite form to certain psychic contents.[1]

Jung defined the collective unconscious as the realm of instincts and archetypes. What do we understand by instincts and archetypes? What is their relationship to each other, and their function in the psyche?

ein word/ das nie gesproch ward·
ein licht/ das no² nie leuchtete·
eine verwir² sondergleich·
v² eine strase ohn' ende·

Jung, C.G. Liber Novus," (The Red Book) 1930–1930, plate 55.

Instinct and archetype influence each other intimately. Instinct is responsible for the activation or triggering of a mode of functioning; the archetype is the pattern or underlying structure that the mode of functioning falls into.

Jung explained instinct as being a set of accumulated, inherited patterns which no longer require learning in order to be activated. We have only to observe young children who, at the sight of certain gadgets, have an automatic ability when it comes to technical skills, even where no learning has taken place. The gadget provides an image, which activates a process which is then triggered into action. Jung defines instincts as "motive forces." Instinctive perception activates; archetypal patterns unfold.

"An image can be considered archetypal when it can be shown to exist in the records of human history in identical form and with the same meaning."[2]

Archetypes have many forms but also distinct features. One particular archetype portrayed in mythology is the hero. The hero with his typical characteristics mobilises energy in the psyche and provides a direction. Adults often remember a first hero model from their childhood. The hero, consciously or unconsciously calls for imitation and provides the model for an ideal and appropriate behaviour. The hero as conqueror with the habitual pattern of descent, confrontation and return, knows the way.

He journeys to unknown realms to confront what is beyond known limits and by so doing he carries development and even evolution a step further. The hero exemplifies the right attitude to situations and therefore represents a model the ego can lean on to enable it to react in the most appropriate manner. Jung says that the psyche cannot evolve without the a priori inborn forms or models that he defined as archetypes. That which recognises and activates the integration of the hero model is instinct.

Often in psychotherapy patients have to learn that they do actually possess instinct and that instinct can be relied upon as a force. Instinct also determines the natural drive for the realisation of the personality as a whole. Despite the fact that instinct, being unconscious, is often ignored and not relied upon, it is always present, except in severely pathological cases. Instinct reacts at the appropriate time, to the right word or image. When a therapist is confronted with the problems of the patient the first task is therefore not to approach with personal ideas but to see what the unconscious of the person has to say about their own situation and where instinct and the unconscious will lead to. Access to the unconscious is essential for consciousness to accompany instinct. As we have seen, access is acquired through dreams, active imaginations and spontaneous drawing.

In any analytical process the psyche may initially be preoccupied with personal unconscious dreams, dreams which respond to the ego, its position or attitude and recognisable life situations. Eventually one comes to a level where dreams seem to come from another realm, from some deeper level in the psyche.

The collective unconscious manifests itself in the individual life through what the Amerindians call "big dreams." These dreams are impersonal, meaning that they do not necessarily reflect details of the person's ordinary life or daily preoccupations. They are numinous, compelling, intriguing. They may be accompanied by other world images, sensations or feelings. They are most often considered healing dreams or dreams that carry a message for the life of the individual. They may also overwhelm a fragile ego or determine an unusual behaviour. Some "big dreams" may remain in the person's memory all through life.

In the collective psyche fairy tales and myths lead on into the deeper levels of the unconscious via the forest, underground realms, the land of the beyond, or dark journeying on the night sea. Once in the unconscious, assuming confrontation requires a certain type of behaviour, as reacting to what we encounter in the right manner can lead to liberation from the previous situation or complex. The result is progression to a new stage of development with a renewed attitude and newfound possibilities of life. The simpleton isn't so naïve anymore; through his experience he has acquired authority, a more mature attitude and a stronger sense of self.

Fairy tales and myths satisfy an instinctive need by demonstrating how the unconscious participates in the unfolding and resolution of life's enigmas. One has to learn that the overall determining factor is not the ego and rational thinking, but the collaboration with the unexpected intelligence of the unconscious. The process described in myths is akin to the process we discover in the unconscious, and this becomes especially clear, as we shall see through a series of spontaneous drawings.

Notes

1 Jung, *CW* Vol. 8, pp. 43, 90.
2 Jung, *CW* Vol. 5, p. 77, para. 114.

Chapter Seven

The transcendent function

According to Jung, joining consciousness with unconscious contents leads the way to a transcendent state. This dynamic, where conscious and unconscious contents come to meet, eventually leads to what Jung defined as the "transcendent function": "*With the unconscious and conscious standpoints the confrontation of the two positions generates a tension charged with energy and creates a living third thing, not a logical stillbirth . . . but a movement out of the suspension between the opposites, a living birth that leads to a new level of being, a new situation.*"[1]

The transcendent function is an unconscious phenomenon which takes place spontaneously in the depths of the psyche when the ego is brought into interaction with unconscious material. The interrelating of ego and unconscious is an important aspect in any analytical process or quest for self-development. According to Jung: "*Consciousness is continually widened through the confrontation of previously unconscious contents, or – to be more accurate – could be widened if it took the trouble to integrate them.*"[2]

The transcendent function belongs naturally to every psychic process and takes place throughout life when transitions are being made from one stage of development to another, or from one level of consciousness to a higher, more mature level. This transcendence may be well illustrated in a series of drawings where the change from one state or attitude to another becomes clear.

The transcendent function is mediated by symbols which have both conscious and unconscious aspects, as well as by instincts and archetypes. Giving one's whole attention to the symbolism and amplifying it, elaborating on it, can bring one to the gold of transformation through this particular function.

The process requires relating to, rather than analysing the material. "*It is not abso-lutely necessary for the process of confrontation itself to become conscious in every detail.*"[3] However, this does have an effect on conscious apprehension and eventually leads to understanding. Jung says: "*Once the unconscious content has been given form and the meaning of the formulation is understood, the question arises as to how the ego will relate to this position, and how the ego and the unconscious are to come to terms.*"[4]

Of course he prescribes that the ego treat the material coming from the uncon-scious with respect and credibility even if it appears at first irrational and incom-patible with the habitual manner of thinking. He says the ego relates in two ways, rationally or creatively. This means one can take a purely rational approach to the psychological event or just confide the material to the creative instinct by drawing, painting or any other artistic activity. The integration of unconscious contents and the ego's adequate attitude are the criteria for the transcendent function to take place.

Jung used the method of amplification to stimulate the production of this function. The transcendent function remains an unconscious phenomenon which requires intuitive perception to be felt or perceived. As it takes place outside of consciousness its effects may be produced but not consciously apprehended. It does however carry with it a sense of well-being, release and change. One may wake up in the morning feeling refreshed and not be aware of what has been going on in the unconscious during the night to produce such a state. "*The secret participation of the unconscious is everywhere present without our having to search for it, but as it remains unconscious we never really know what is going on or what to expect.*"[5]

What is the difference in the approach to the child and the approach to the adult or the more mature ego? As the child's consciousness is limited in the face of uncon-scious material and in some regard, he must also be protected from overwhelming unconscious images, the analyst becomes the conscious container and mediator of the transcendent function. The analyst is also the one who at the same time relies on the child's instinct coming from the intimate source of the self within. In cases of weakened egos, the analyst can be the model for the ego to lean on and thereby develop the means of dealing with the material. This is because the analyst has the appropriate attitude to the unconscious and can in a sense become the alter ego – the carrier of consciousness, somewhat like the hero.

The following is a spontaneous story produced in a session by nine-year-old Amy who suffers from feelings of rejection amongst her peers and complains of isolation and loneliness.

A little girl is out on a walk with her Furry Friend when she suddenly happens upon an unknown grotto. With the help of her Furry Friend she discovers a mysterious key . . .

Curious about where the key belongs she decides to penetrate into the dark grotto.

Once there, she and Furry Friend suddenly jump with fright, as they are confronted by a flame-spitting monster who dwells in the grotto. They disturbed him by their intrusion.

The monster spits fire but Furry Friend has spotted something in the background which he believes may be helpful in this situation.

The little girl gathers all her courage and faces the monster armed with the magical sword that gives her unexpected power. Furry Friend does the same.

She plunges her sword into the heart of the monster with all her might and kills him. Furry Friend did his best to help and injured the monster whilst she took care of the rest.

Beyond the monster lay a huge treasure chest which she hopes the key may belong to. All her fears fade away as she discovers unexpected riches.

She covers herself in jewels and gold before leaving the grotto . . .

…and returns to the school yard where she shares all her riches with the other children.

We can see that "Furry Friend," the helping animal, represents some instinct in this child that was mobilised helping her to confront her fears and acquire the appropriate means to transcend to another level of development. The symbolism of the sword would relate to the taking up of a decisive and clear attitude to cut through fears and complexes. Killing the monster through active participation and confrontation led to transcendence.

Amy did return to the real schoolyard that had previously been the place of her most acute fears and where she had felt incapable of facing others. Her renewed sense of self soon became evident when she began to make friends and was no longer hovering on the edge as before. The idea of sharing brought with it a sense of openness and a deep desire to connect. Amy who was fundamentally of an altruistic nature began to express this and became more confident in her newfound extraversion. The new treasure for her was to transcend from a neurotic fearful state to an open and expressive way of being.

For Jung, "*The treatment of neurosis is not a kind of psychological water cure, but a renewal of the personality, working in every direction and penetrating every sphere of life.*"[6]

Notes

1 Jung, *CW* Vol. 8, pp. 90, 89.
2 Ibid. p. 91, para. 193.
3 Ibid. p. 89, para. 188.
4 Ibid. p. 87, para. 181.
5 Ibid. p. 79, para. 158.
6 Ibid. p. 88, para. 184.

Chapter Eight

Alfonso and "The Red Toad"

I met Alfonso when I was in charge of a drawing class which took place once a week with a group of children between seven and eight years old. Prior to our first meeting I had no knowledge of Alfonso's background or family history. His drawings however did eventually attract my attention more than any other in the group.

Alfonso is a bright-eyed, blond child of eight years and, despite a certain reserve, he participates well in the class.

This is his first drawing, which he entitled "The Labyrinth."

As the labyrinth occupies the central place in the drawing we can relate its position to the ego of the child. But what could it mean for the ego of a child to be caught in a labyrinth? The labyrinth is brown, confirming its underworld, chthonic aspect. In myth it is the place where the hero, the model for the conscious ego, must descend to meet that which lies in the beyond. But what does that mean for the psyche of an eight-year-old child? What actually does lie in the beyond, in the unknown spheres of the unconscious of this child?

Considering that the labyrinth is a symbol for the underworld, one can anticipate that the psychic energy of this child is not connected to outer everyday events but to the unconscious and its images. We can also recognise the tendency towards regression in the theme of the drawing, which is in an inner room, looking out onto a barren mountain of a colourless and empty world. When the outer world is empty, the inner world becomes activated and motifs take on meaning.

In Alfonso's inner world he includes a cat, a symbol of eros, feeling, relatedness and anima instinct. But this cat is cut off, isolated on its cushion. The cat has no paws, no means of contacting the world and therefore has a sad, forlorn, expression.

On the bottom right is what Alfonso calls "the door to the labyrinth," once again repeating the motif and amplifying its importance.

The first drawing invites us into an inner realm where the libido or psychic energy is in a state of regression, and where we expect inner images may become even more alive.

"The Bear and the Honey."

In this drawing, which Alfonso produced one week later, we seem to have gone through the window of drawing No.1 and have arrived at the place of the mountain. Alfonso tells me that this drawing is about the bear who seeks the honey – but the honey seems far away, in the beyond. One wonders: is the honey attainable, or not?

He also describes the sun as a sinking sun, thus indicating a state where the light above recedes and the lower realms of the unconscious become illuminated. We can see a plus sign on the left, and a minus sign on the right conscious sphere, indicating once again that the energy in the unconscious is positive and is directed towards regression and the underworld. One wonders what is happening in the outer world in the life of this child. Do Alfonso's next drawings give us any indication?

"Journeying in a Submarine."

The image gives us little hope that the fox, symbolising this child's instinct, can have any influence on the submarine's inevitable descent. If we had any doubts about the movement of the psychic energy, we are now convinced of its direction as we see the submarine making its way towards the deepest waters. The periscope with its fragile fox seems to throw a last glance towards the shore.

"The Three Nests." (facing page)

"The Three Nests" was the title Alfonso spontaneously gave to this fourth drawing. But these nests are all precariously positioned, two of them on a lopped-off tree branch, and the third on a steep cliff face.

If we look closely at the nests, we can also see that they contain eggs, but none that could possibly come to maturity. The only colour in the drawing, green, the colour of nature and life, seems to be evaporating out of the only nest which could have given us hope. The nests may be considered as mandalas, but these mandalas are incomplete, broken and not reflective of any life-giving element. These nests may be considered to be disturbed mandalas.

Jung says:

There are conditions when one sees disturbed mandalas . . . in them a proper circle will suddenly come to an end, a break will occur, disturbing the whole thing, and then it is just as if part of what belonged there had been cut away and strange elements have been substituted. Such a drawing represents a state of possession or obsession in which people harbour strange ghosts in their psychology.[1]

Is this broken mandala a symbol of a state of possession and invasion in Alfonso's case? But what could be invading the psyche of this child and preventing him from having a healthy access to life and the environment? A child's nest is also his home and family and one can begin to be curious about Alfonso's home situation. As yet, there is no information.

We do not know what is happening in the life of this child that is blocking the outward flow of energy, but we do know that the inner world is highly activated and that the unconscious is living a process which is vividly expressed through Alfonso's drawings. The process taking place within the psyche of this child is undoubtedly dynamic. Despite several long periods without drawing class due to holidays and long weekends, the unconscious remained coherent and maintained the red thread of the theme of regression and continuity through the symbolical representations. Jung says that psychic energy seeks its own goal. What could this goal possibly be?

Alfonso then produced this drawing, which he told me is of a "Red Toad."

Alfonso seems to be very well versed on red toads, which he says come from Indonesia and are poisonous. So here we have the image of the monster from the depths, which is devouring the bee, the symbol of life. The submarine and the little fox journeyed to the depths and there found an image of the destroyer of life who has been lurking in the dark, lying dormant, dwelling in the under layers of the psyche of this child.

Now that a beam of the light of consciousness has been shed upon the red toad, a battle can begin. Images are concrete and can be confronted. The ego has become conscious of the monster and the form the unconscious has given it. It is a case of what Jung calls "instinct perceiving it." The complex inhabiting the psyche sucking its life force and blocking a normal progression has taken on shape and form. Now the challenge is either to be devoured by being so fascinated by the images that the energy gets stuck in the unconscious and is no longer available for life and development; or to take up arms and struggle for freedom from the luring depths as every hero in myth must do.

Will the ego of this child decide to sink or surface from the depths? Will he have the strength to battle for release from the luring attraction of the inner world? What does it require to surface again and allow the libido to free itself from the inner pull? As Alfonso shows me his drawing I perceive a telling glint in his eye; his excitement and enthusiasm betray a real fascination for the toad of his unconscious. For any analyst this is an alarming scenario.

Jung quotes Goethe's Faust: "*Yet the danger is great,*" as Mephistopheles says, "*for these depths fascinate.*"[2]

He says:

> *Whenever some great work is to be accomplished, before which a man recoils, doubtful of his strength, his libido streams back to the fountainhead – and that is the dangerous moment when the issue hangs between annihilation and new life. For if the libido gets stuck in the wonderland of this inner world, then for the upper world man is nothing but a shadow, he is already moribund or seriously ill. But if the libido manages to tear itself loose and force its way up again, something like a miracle happens: the journey to the underworld was a plunge into the fountain of youth, and the libido apparently dead, wakes to a renewed fruitfulness.*[3]

We can surmise that Alfonso has reached the point where the ego can lose its outer world orientation and get lost in the attraction to inner images. When the ego turns its attention towards the inner image substituting it for real life, it may no longer have the strength to resist the pull, at which point it becomes invaded and submerged by inner representations that have no reference to reality and the developmental life of a child. But what can possibly influence a state of fascination?

Jung says: "*Practical experience teaches us, as a general rule, that a psychic activity can find a substitute only on the basis of equivalence. A pathological interest, for example, an intense attachment to a symptom, (or image), can be replaced only by an equally intense attachment to another interest, which is why a release of libido from the symptom never takes place without a substitute.*"[4]

I realise that the attraction is powerful and that a substitute is imminently necessary. But what could that substitute be? And Alfonso is not in analysis; I only see him once a week in a drawing class.

My concern increases when he presents his next drawing, which he calls the "Night owl."

"Night owl."

Alfonso informs me that the mouse at the bottom right wants to get to the hole on the left. If we take the images seriously, it is clear from his drawing that the mouse is in a truly precarious situation and the prognosis for its successful escape seems rather poor.

At this point I decide to tell the class the story of Theseus, the Greek hero, whose fate was to descend into the labyrinth of Minos in Crete and confront the Minotaur, who was devouring the youth and life-force of Athens. For Theseus, as for any hero, the passage through the labyrinth corresponds to an initiation, and successful completion of the journey leads to psychic liberation, a strengthening of the ego, a renewed sense of self, and a step up to a new level of development.

Theseus, as hero, knows the way. Joseph Campbell says: "*We have not even to risk the adventure alone; for the heroes of all time have gone before us; the labyrinth is thoroughly known; we have only to follow the thread of the hero-path.*"[5]

The real benefit of journeying on the path of descent and re-emergence is freedom from the dominant complex which was stocked in the unconscious and inhibited access to life. Theseus as an archetypal image can influence at a deep intra-psychic level. The hero archetype provides the model for the ego's development and growth. I could see that the myth held the attention of Alfonso, who rather liked mythology and stories.

But this is the end of term. There will be no more classes and I will not be seeing Alfonso again. The teacher had tried to approach his mother on the subject of therapy for Alfonso because of the poverty of his schoolwork, but she declared that "therapy would only steal his soul," and the answer was a definite "no."

I ask Alfonso what he is doing for his holidays and he tells me he is going to Sicily and that he is especially interested in the volcano, and the Roman ruins. My heart sinks as the power of these symbols flashes across my mind. Volcanoes explode and burst forth from below as does psychosis; ruins symbolically reflect the fragmentation the ego can fall into when this explosion occurs. I suddenly had the feeling that I could seek further to attempt to find a form of equivalence. I ask Alfonso if he has any dreams.

"Oh! Yes!" he replies, and spontaneously tells me a recent dream: "I'm with Starsky and Hutch. We are driving to a place where we go into a building and take a lift to an upper floor. There we drink a beer together. Later we return to the car and drive off."

As Jung says; "*How can we presume to want to know in advance from where the light will come to us?*"[6]

It is now clear that the equivalence has been found in the person of the hero archetype in a more modern, humanised form, which is nearer to consciousness. Starsky and Hutch, "the invincibles," are providing the model for the transportation of psychic energy which may now progress and bring the ego of this child back to the concrete world. The lift going up indicates that the libido has shifted and is moving upwards towards progression. We now hope that the toad of the depths can be conquered and recede forever.

But this is the last day of term and we are on the doorsteps of the school. There will be no more drawing classes and summer holidays have just begun. Fearing that Alfonso may lose contact with his newfound hero images, I wonder how the potential can be maintained in the psyche of this child. I ask Alfonso if he can draw his dream. "Oh! Yes!" he says with enthusiasm, "drawing class was the best class I have ever been to!"

As I descend the steps leaving the school, it is as if I perceive for the first time that this child with his pale blue eyes, his porcelain features and his floppy blond curls does indeed possess something of a young god, perhaps the fate of one too.

At the beginning of the autumn term, eight weeks later, I received the following drawing through the post, carefully packed and well protected.

"Starsky and Me!"

Here, as we can readily see, there has been a distinct change in direction, the psychic energy has shifted and maintained its tendency towards a progressive flow. The paving stones become stronger as the energy drives forward. The hero is present; the ego has won the battle with the elements from the depths and has returned to a humanised fantasy world and, one may presume, to concrete life. As I was feeling the effect of the drawing, I had no doubt of who was at the wheel of Starsky's car.

I was most curious to see the mass of grey on the left where the shutters on the barren empty world are now closed, where the castrating owl has faded nearly into oblivion and where the mouse has finally reached its hole. Conscious memory could not have retained these symbols with such precision but the unconscious did its work, maintaining the red thread of coherence over and beyond time lapses, interferences and other events in a most effective manner.

Now I can have confidence in Alfonso's inner strength and his power to overcome depression, regression and annihilation. The turning point where libido has shifted from regression to progression has been achieved; his process is now tending towards life and natural growth. Alfonso has been initiated, his ego has travelled the way of the hero, and life with all its challenges awaits him.

The owl with its castrating claws is a symbol of Hecate and Athena. We notice that we are confronted with a striking absence of masculine symbols. The owl was on the verge of killing the reduced masculine identity of this child. A castration complex may come from the parental attitude towards this child, an overpowering possessive mother figure, but it seems also that the lack of any masculine symbols would suggest lack of possibility of identifying with a healthy masculine counterpart in the outer world. Starsky did what other humans in the immediate environment failed to do: provide the model for development of the ego of this young boy.

Connecting with the Starsky image provided a source of energy which allowed the battle to take place. Jung says; "*A suggestion is never accepted without an inner readiness for it, or if after great insistence it is accepted, it is immediately lost again. A suggestion that is accepted for any length of time always presupposes a marked psychological readiness which is merely brought into play by the so-called suggestion.*"[7]

Alfonso came to terms with his own unconscious myth. Jung points to the need "*to come to a real settlement with the unconscious.*" He says this is of course something very different from interpretation. "*But in the case of a real settlement it is not a question of interpretation: it is a question of releasing unconscious processes and letting them come into the conscious mind in the form of fantasies.*" He says, "*I would not give priority to the understanding. For the important thing is not to interpret and understand the fantasies but primarily to experience them.*"[8]

And this is what Alfonso did through his drawings. He accompanied the living myth that his own unconscious provided.

Notes

1 Jung, *Vision Seminars*, p. 103.
2 von Goethe's *Faust* part 1, *CW* Vol. 5, p. 293, para. 449.
3 Jung C.G, *CW* Vol. 5, pp. 292–293, para. 449.

4   Jung C.G. *CW* Vol. 8, p. 21, para. 39.
5   Campbell, J. *The Hero with a Thousand Faces*, Bollingen series XVII, Princeton University Press, 1973, p. 25.
6   Jung, *Liber Novus*, p. 237.
7   Jung, *CW* Vol. 8, p. 75, para. 150.
8   Jung, C.G. *CW* Vol. 7, Bollingen series, Princeton University Press, 1953, 1972, p. 213, para. 342.

Chapter Nine

Totemism

Since the night of time man has had a deep and intimate connection with the animal kingdom. Once upon a time man was so completely in tune with nature and the elements that he found it necessary to incorporate the spirit and qualities of the animals, so as to attain physical and supernatural powers. Cohesion in native societies involved imitation of animal characteristics and behaviours. Clans base their identity on animal attributes. In North America, the native people define themselves as members of the raven clan, the crow clan, the beaver clan and so on.

The shaman, the Amerindian, or the native from any indigenous culture, seeks to know and incorporate the powers of his animal totem. He must first and foremost establish as part of his unique personality a spiritual connection with his power animal. The discovery of his corresponding totem comes from a revelation in dreams or a privileged encounter in nature.

Jung declared his own affinity with the animal kingdom: *"Because they are so closely akin to us and share our unknowingness, I loved all warm-blooded animals who have souls like ourselves and with whom, so I thought, we have an instinctive understanding."*[1]

The psychic or spiritual connection with the totem animal brings with it the particular attributes and capacities that characterise the specific animal. One is far more powerful when one has psychically incorporated one's totem. One becomes an integral part of nature and an initiated participant in the mysteries of the elements. Subsequently the right to hunt may be bestowed or the right to avail oneself of the essences in nature for one's own development, maturation and well-being.

"My Lion" by a nine-year-old girl

Barbara Hannah, a close collaborator of Jung states:

Like native peoples, Jung felt that the animal was sublime, that it was indeed the "divine" side of the human psyche. Animals live much more in contact with a "secret" order within nature itself and far more than man – they live closely connected with the "absolute knowledge" of the unconscious. In contradistinction to man, the animal is the living being that follows its own inner laws beyond good and evil. And herein lies the superiority of the animal.[2]

Can it be possible that this absolute knowledge of the unconscious is still a reality and is revealed through the animal images coming from the depths of the psyche even today? What seems to be evident is the fact that a spontaneous drawing, through animal images, reveals something other, less rational, than a consciously produced drawing.

One particularly well-known exercise is to portray the family in drawing and then as a second exercise to draw the family as animals.

"My family" by a six-year-old girl.

And then "My Family as animals" by the same child.

What is the difference? What is more revealing in the animal representations then in the more conscious images?

And "This is my family" by another six-year-old girl.

"I'm the wolf, my Dad's a wolf like me, but he is red. Mom is a butterfly."
"And who is the goldfish?"
"My brother of course!"

So here we find a strong identification with the father and a certain exclusion of the mother who is not of the same realm.

Then we have the drawing of the little brother who did not see his sister's drawing.

"The goldfish on the left is me," he affirms, *"my sister is the cat."*

It is interesting to note that the little brother also draws himself as a goldfish, not, however, in a bowl! But then one wonders, what do cats do with goldfish? And how does a goldfish, that can't go further than his bowl, deal with a cat?

These two children are in fact twins and it is clear that the unconscious projection of the sister is revealing itself, but how much is it overwhelming and determining the brother's sense of self and identity? We know that projection on the child contributes to the development of his narcissism and self worth. This is obviously a case to be investigated to see what is going on between the two and within the family dynamic. The identification with the father seems to point to sibling jealousy and rivalry for the father's attention.

Despite our modernity, we haven't lost the connection to the animal world, which is part of our inheritance, and which has an accumulated identity in the psyche of mankind since the night of time. Myths and fairy tales, as expressions of our own collective unconscious, abound with animal motifs, encounters and animal wiles. The bird knows the way, the fox has the cunning to get past the obstacle, the eagle sees beyond the human range, the duck can dive and retrieve what is lost, and the frog and the toad are magically transformed. Animal capacities in myths and fairy tales are limitless.

Barbara Hannah also wrote: "*The study of the symbolism of animals is indeed a great need of our age, for animals represent various aspects of instincts, and our time is notoriously badly divorced from instincts.*"[3]

She goes on to say: "*We measure the distance from consciousness by whether the animal is warm or cold-blooded, vertebrate or non-vertebrate, and so on. Animals in general represent these dim luminosities and they are able to guide us in places where our ego consciousness would be powerless.*"[4]

Evolutionary scale of symbols

Personal unconscious level
Humanised characters, shadowy figures, fantasy figures
Intermediary levels
Anthropomorphic animal, gods & goddesses, animal forms, from smallest to biggest
Deeper levels
Cold-blooded forms, frogs, toads, reptiles
Non-vertebrates
Snails, snakes, eels, etc.
Mythological levels
Dinosaurs, monsters, gargoyles and dragons

In the very distant past man devoted himself religiously to his connection with the animal realm. In the Palaeolithic caves of France, where the art forms go back as far as 35,000 years, the drawings and paintings are almost uniquely devoted to animals. Visiting these caves awakens a deep sense of awe and participation. The atmosphere of something "other" is so alive that one feels the effect of this living experience that has crossed the millennia beyond time and space: 35,000 years distance has done nothing to stamp out the impenetrable "numen" that reigns in these ancient sites that were so revered by our ancestors and where the representation of the animals had priority over all.

Font-de-Gaume, Dordogne, France.

"My family as animals" by six-year-old Dody; "*I'm the elk*," he affirms!

Notes

1   Jaffé and Jung, *Memories*, p. 67.
2   Hannah, B. *The Archetypal Symbolism in Animals Lectures Given at the C.G. Jung Institute, Zurich, 1954–1958*, Chiron Publication, 2006, p.VIII.
3   Ibid. p.VII.
4   Ibid. p. 141.

Chapter Ten

Bobby and "The Fish"

Bobby was an angry young boy when I met him. At 12 years old he was angry with his parents, his peers, the world and especially his school. In fact, Bobby hadn't been to school for the past six months and, despite an obviously high IQ and efficient home schooling, he wasn't making the grade.

Bobby had no friends, had never been invited home by any of his peers during his school years, and was socially very isolated. The days were long and boring. Beyond the anger Bobby was a sad and lonely boy, although sadness could not be admitted. Anger was the shield that protected Bobby from his own deep despair. With feet on the desk, staring out of pale grey eyes, Bobby kept a defiant silence as he sat across from me. It was a silence that I felt appropriate to respect.

"*I didn't want to come here,*" he eventually blurted. "*They forced me to, and I won't do anything!*"

"*I guess if I were you I would feel the same.*" I returned. This seemed to break the ice.

"*What are you anyway? One of those 'psy' somethings? I've seen ten of them and they are all no good.*"

I allowed the tension to flow out of Bobby as he ranted and complained. Eventually I said, passing a blank page across the desk, "*Draw me a tree.*"

Bobby had the choice of crayons, pastels, coloured pencils, etc., but as his choice fell on the lead pencil, I just observed.

This was Bobby's tree drawing.

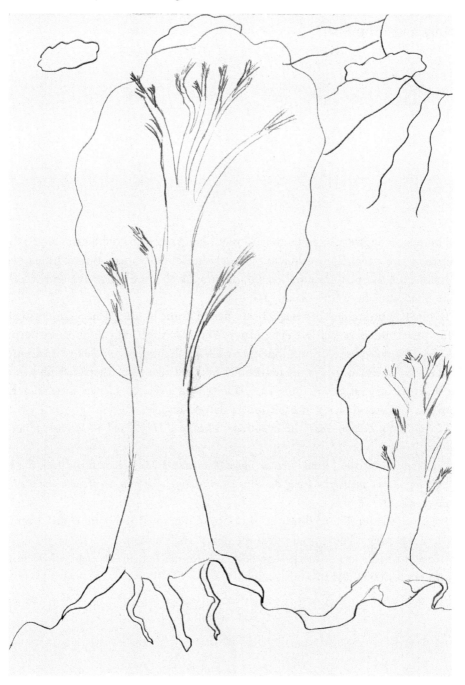

Bobby also drew "a person" revealing a depleted and weakened sense of self.

At the end of our first session Bobby's mother said in passing: *"Oh! By the way I have kept all of Bobby's drawings since he began to draw at the age of three-and-a-half years old."*

The following week I spread Bobby's drawings on the living room floor and sifted through hundreds of pages of scribbles, shapes and themes. Bobby's earliest drawings, which he began at the age of three-and-a-half years old, illustrated a repetition of the following theme.

There were dozens of these motifs spread out on the floor before me. Jung's words began ringing in my head; *". . . there are things in the psyche which I do not produce, but which produce themselves and have their own life."*[1]

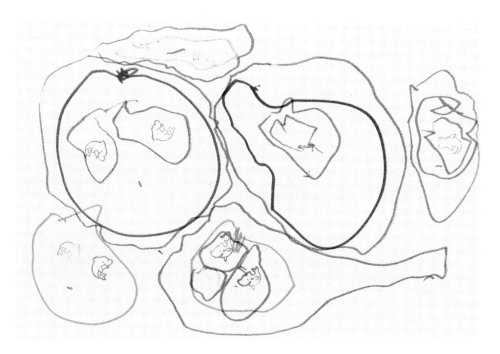

Bobby's mother had written on the back of the drawings that this theme had begun at the beginning of her third pregnancy and had been repeated from the age of three-and-a-half to four-and-a-half years old when drawing on the theme suddenly ceased.

When an image, a number, or a theme, repeats itself, it indicates that psyche is insisting on something that has not become conscious, or has not had enough conscious attention. What was the unconscious of a three-and-a-half-year-old trying to express?

The mother had written on the back of this drawing called "The Fish":

"*Blue is to protect the fish from the hunters.*"

At the bottom of this drawing there is a little fellow trying to hold the whole mass up with obvious effort and difficulty.

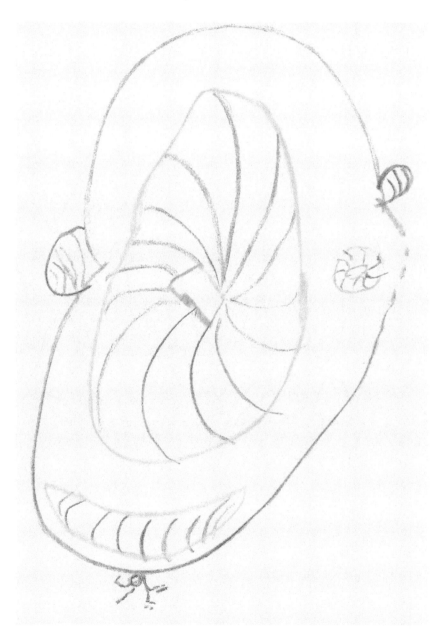

Is something becoming more distinct as the child advances in age and ability?

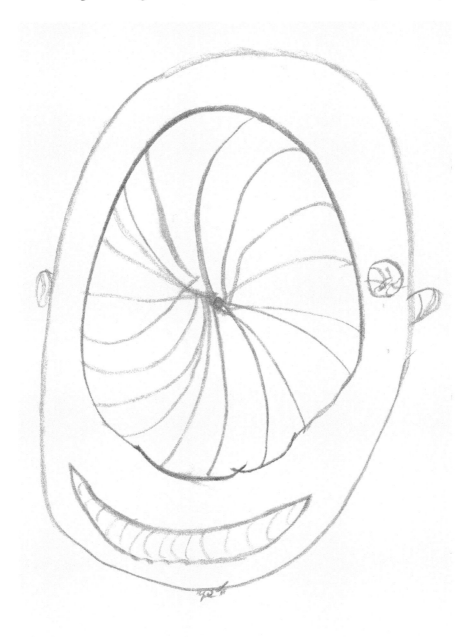

When I show these drawings to Bobby, consciously he has a vague memory of them. But Bobby's unconscious has a "real" memory of them.

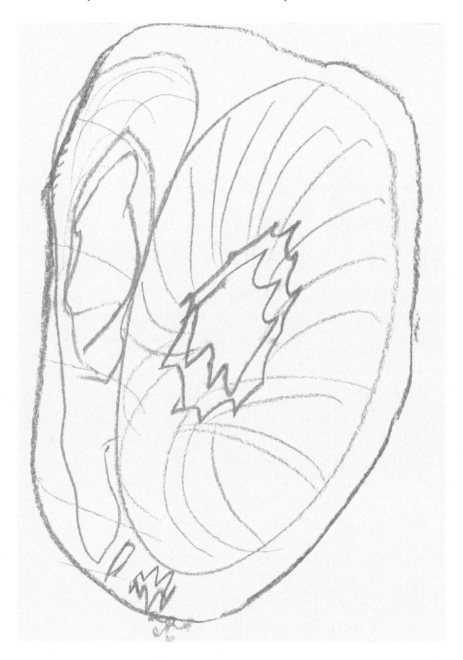

Confusion reigns.

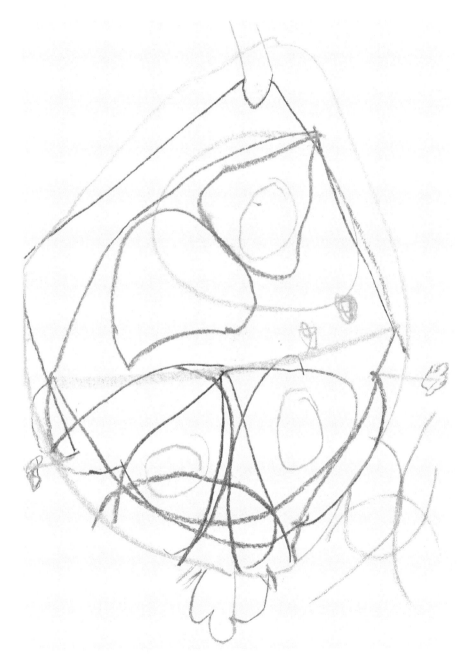

Bobby spontaneously describes this next drawing as a skull-and-cross-bones.

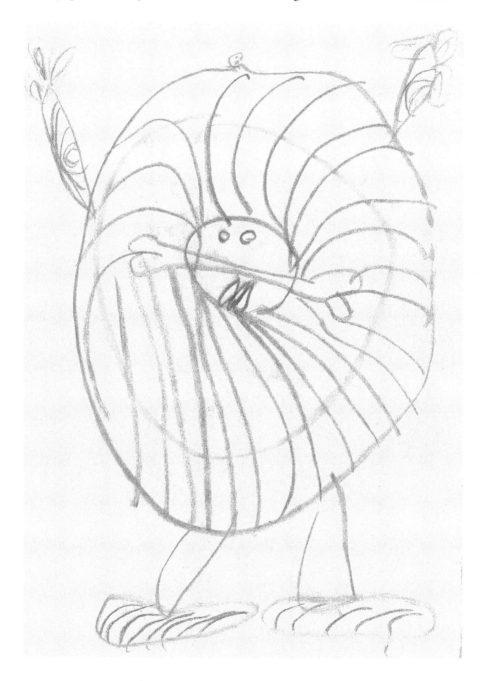

Eventually we find the original fish as in the very first drawings accompanied by a smaller fish with another heart.

The double heart repeats itself once again and in several drawings.

Until one day . . . there is only one heart.

The heart has received a severe shock: an electrocuted heart.
A heart is sinking back to its origin in the blue of the ocean of the unconscious . . .

It eventually sinks on the horizon and leaves forever . . .

This leaves a child with a sensation of separation, depression and loss.

But the sensation of an explosion has remained in the psyche of this young boy and seems responsible for the split between himself and the world around him.

Now we see clearly what the tree drawing refers to. The second tree doesn't have the same potential for growth but remains attached to the stronger tree as if trying to claim enough strength for life.

This was Bobby's last tree drawing.

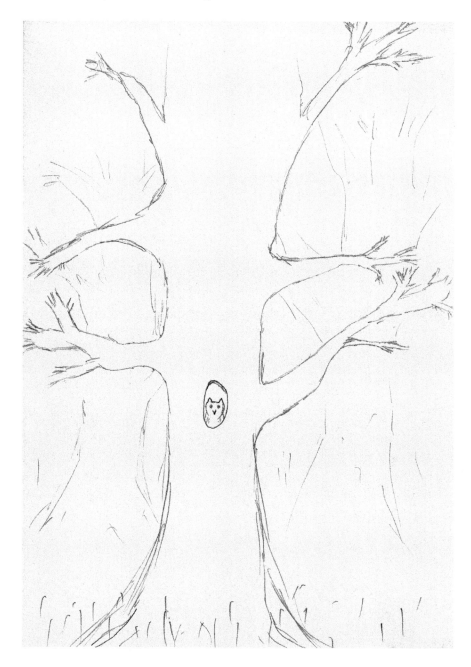

Although there is some unlived life yet to be compensated for, Bobby's new tree now has only one trunk, and recollections of the past don't seem to inhibit growth anymore.

Bobby remembers when he was six years old seeing a vision of another boy on the stairs in his house. The boy was like himself.

Does this refer to a return of Bobby's "sense of self" to himself, or is it an objective reality that Bobby had actually accompanied another self, in the womb before birth? Jung says the objective and subjective viewpoints are both real; the feeling tone may be equivalent whether it corresponds to an outer, or an inner, reality. The effect of the reliving of these images in our sessions allowed Bobby to go through a conscious mourning process. Bobby had always had a strong sensation of a "loss of the other" and a "search for his other half" in life.

Slowly but surely, Bobby returned to school. He gradually picked up on social life and found friends. The first time Bobby was invited to a birthday party was an important event which marked a turning point for him.

Eventually Bobby met another young boy of his own age with whom he became close friends. Bobby and Benny lived an intense and creative time together inventing stories and adventures and even making films that they composed and posted on the net. Bobby was very proud of their productions.

Today Bobby is socially and academically in the throes of creative living. His passion has turned to music and he is recognised and acclaimed for his talents.

Some years later Benny left for the other side of the world and Bobby came back for a few sessions. Next summer Bobby will journey to the other side of the world too. Meaningful relationships may well endure beyond separation and distances.

Our basis is ego consciousness, our world the field of light centred upon the focal point of the ego. From that point we look out upon an enigmatic world of obscurity never knowing to what extent the shadowy forms we see are caused by our consciousness or possess a reality of their own. The superficial observer is content with the first assumption. But closer study shows that as a rule the images of the unconscious are not produced by consciousness, but have a reality and spontaneity of their own.[2]

Notes
1 Jaffé and Jung, *Memories*, p. 207.
2 Ibid. p. 324.

ein word / das nie gesprochen ward ·
ein licht / das noch nie leuchtete ·
eine verweis sondergleich ·
vn̄ eine straße ohn' ende ·

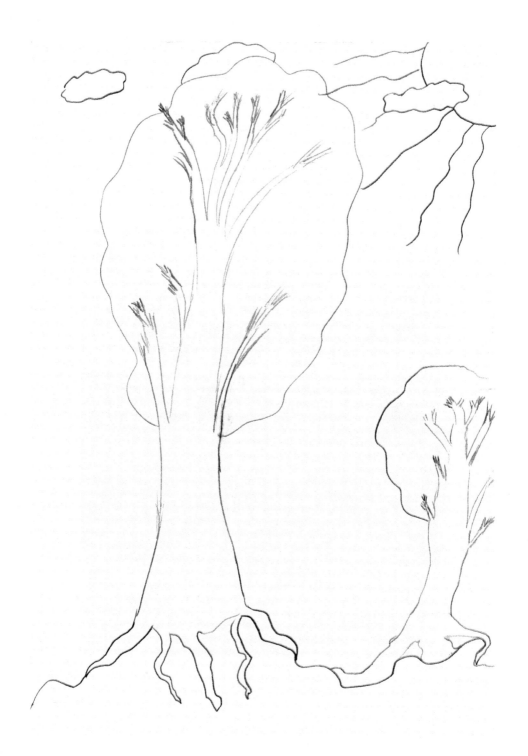

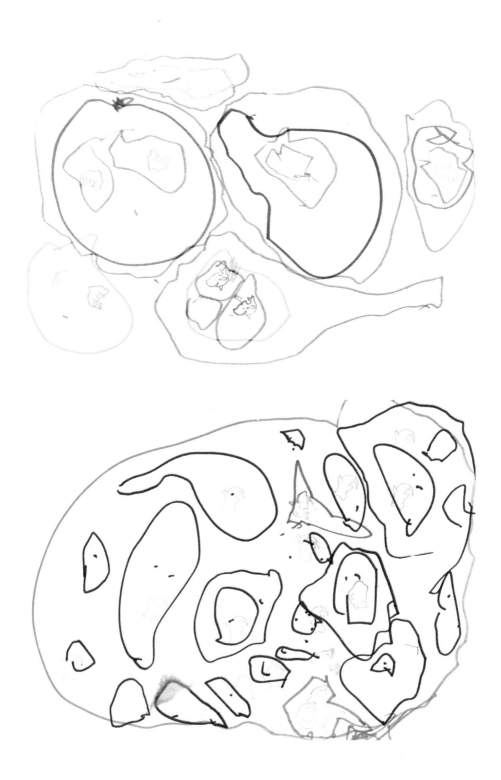

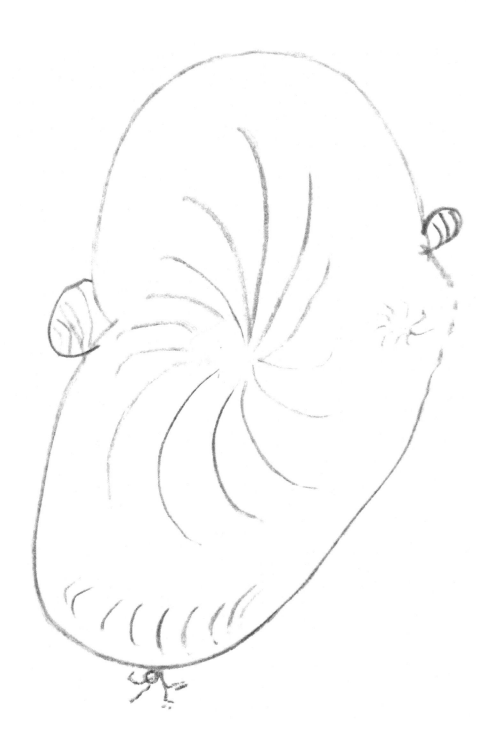

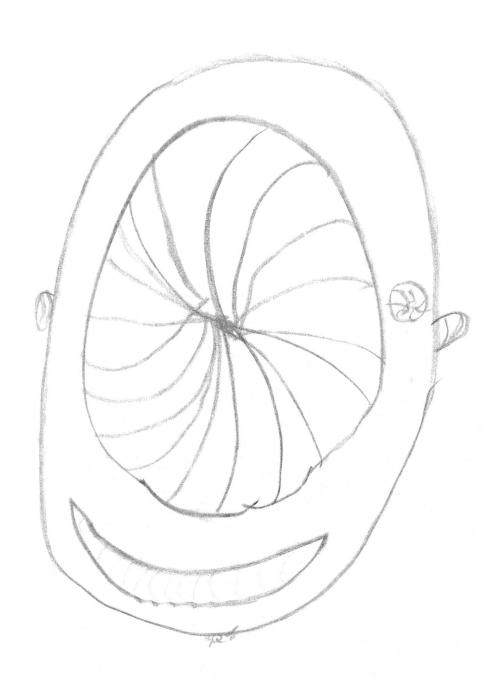

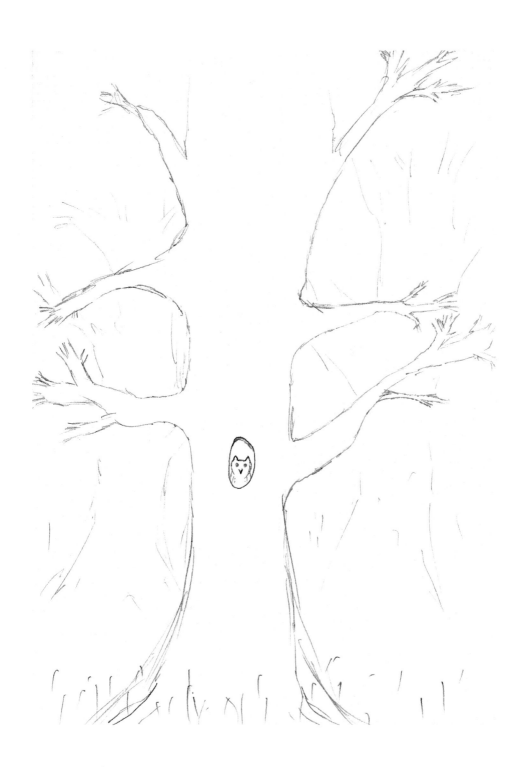

Chapter Eleven

The tree drawing

Since early childhood Jung had an instinctive affinity for nature, the trees and the forests. He says; *"Trees in particular were mysterious and seemed to me direct embodiments of the incomprehensible meaning of life. For that reason, the woods were the place where I felt closest to its deepest meaning and to its awe-inspiring workings."*[1]

The tree, or "Tree of Life," corresponds to the drawing of a life story, the unfolding of a process of development. Jung describes the tree symbol as *"the self, depicted as a process of growth."*[2]

He further says: *"Taken on average, the commonest associations to its meaning are growth, life, unfolding of form in a physical and spiritual sense, development, growth from below upwards and from above downwards, the maternal aspect (protection, shade, shelter, nourishing, fruits, source of life, solidity, permanence, firm-rootedness, but also being rooted to the spot), old age, personality and finally death and rebirth."*[3]

The tree being universal is found as a symbol in many religions, fairy tales and mythologies. Every tree drawing is individual, unique and personal but as a symbol the tree is also universal and common to mankind. Jung affirms: *"In spite of the diversity of the tree symbol, a number of basic features may be established."*[4]

The tree, as a symbol of life from its beginning in the roots at its base, through to the present age, tells us about the process of growth in the person. The unconscious places marks on the tree in the form of holes, nests, cut branches, broken or absent roots, falling leaves, blossoming fruits, or flowers, each a symbolic representation of a personal history. Joyful or sad emotions may be illustrated by animals, i.e., birds, squirrels, snakes, etc.

As a child grows and stabilises through an analytical process, the tree may also grow and transform. This is according to the intrinsic character of the symbol, which as a carrier of energy has the power to develop.

The following is the tree drawing of Dilly, a five-year-old who had in her short life moved house five times.

The latest development of the parental situation was that they were getting a divorce and that the mother was moving to another country. Dilly was therefore once again uprooted from her home, her father, her friends and her analysis. Despite the anticipation of another move, after six months of analysis Dilly's tree is getting stronger, showing that she is developing more inner strength and a greater sense of self. This is what we call the evolution of symbols. It is important to observe in a series of drawings how the symbols evolve.

Here, five-year-old Jacky has had two starts in life, one in America and one in Europe. It seems clear that there was no sense of continuity from one environment to the other, just a sense of starting all over again and a lack of roots or solid ground under his feet.

Billy's drawing expresses another aspect which is preoccupying him at an unconscious level. He had recently lost his grandfather to whom he was very close and with whom he even identified. Billy looked like Grandpa, liked to go fishing like Grandpa and would someday become a policeman just like Grandpa, but here we see the tree of life has faded and the spirit of life leaving in the form of the flying bird rising up. We now know that Billy is still in mourning for the loss of his grandfather and we can accompany his process consciously. With the participation of the unconscious the drawing says what Billy cannot describe in words.

With this tree we understand that a child may grow but not expand, not develop his/her own innate potential.

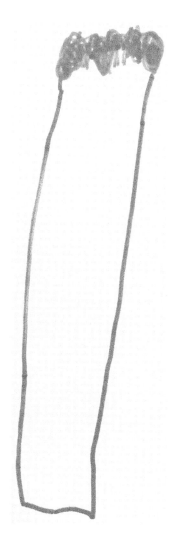

Sometimes attempts at expansion have occurred but have not been brought to fruition as we observe in the stunted growth of the branches of this tree belonging to a 10-year–old.

Tommy at 12 years old had never had a family life and had only known institutions and orphanages. It is clear that he has no sense of roots or stability and psychologically had not had the chance to develop and mature normally. Here Tommy needs to grow roots within himself and find an inner place of security and comfort. Tommy had known three institutions in his lifetime, the three branches, where he had three attempts at finding roots but had not felt at home in any of them. Tommy will be moving shortly to another home.

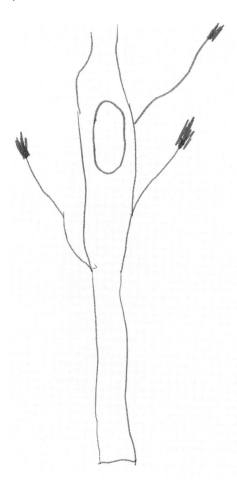

The "feeling tone" in this drawing is one of poverty of expression and lack of engagement.

Alice at 14 years old is very distrustful of anyone who may approach her and especially of anyone who may pry into her past.

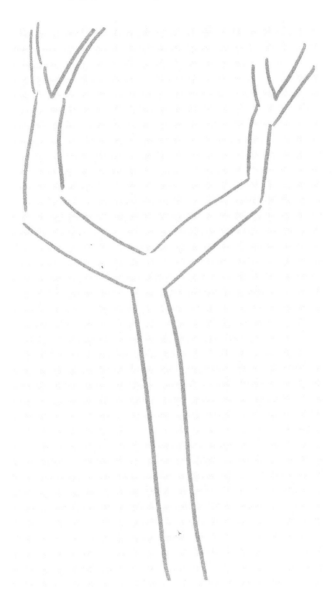

She had been through a long series of emotional and social ruptures in her life which the drawing also portrays in the massive "split" in the tree's development. When this was presented to her as a suggestion of her drawing she immediately made a list of the separations, losses and breakups she had been through. Alice had been three years in a therapeutic centre previous to this first session. As a result of her drawing, and the reality it reflected she began to understand herself at a deep level; she gained confidence in the analytical process and became aware of what was driving her into the chaos of repetitive destructive behaviour patterns. Alice was relieved to discover that a sensation of rupture in her unconscious was the responsible for certain reactions and her repetitive failures. She was then able to change attitude and take up the challenge of the demands of her daily life with energy and commitment. Academically she made a heroic comeback in April of that year and to the surprise of all, succeeded beyond expectations in her June exams.

This tree may look well developed but there is something at the base that has made a significant mark on Mike's life. The four bars in the hole at the bottom refer to the age of four years old, when Mike's mother died. The nine apples refer to a new stage in his life when his father remarried and a new mother was welcomed into the home. The new mother was warm, loving and supportive of Mike while he attempted to find his orientation socially, academically and eventually professionally.

The treetop, however, is not complete, suggesting that Mike feels cut off in his present process and fears of insecurity and loss of ground loom once again.

Mike, who had come merely to discuss his professional orientation, was very surprised by his own drawing and what his unconscious was revealing. He now had the opportunity to consciously accompany an unfinished mourning process which his own unconscious was presenting to him.

On the facing page at top right, we see a bird that has flown the nest flying towards the world and new horizons. There is another one, on the left, just leaving and two more who still remain at home in the middle of the tree.

This drawing belongs to a 43-year-old mother of four who finds herself in the throes of a major transition when her first-born has finally left the nest. With six members in the family, the parents and four children, the eldest has left to pursue his academic career in another country. The unconscious of the mother is preparing her for the flight of a second child, who will soon follow and who is psychologically on her way. What can the parents do apart from support the process and be observers of the unfolding of life's intention for their young?

"The outward form of the tree may change in the course of time, but the richness and vitality of a symbol are expressed more in its change of meaning. The aspect of meaning is therefore essential to phenomenology of the tree symbol."[5]

Checklist for the tree drawing

Tree

From base to treetop, the tree represents the growth from the roots to the summit or from birth to the present. Dividing the tree from the base to tip gives an idea of the age or stage in development when events occurred and registered on the psyche.

How is the tree planted on the ground? Has it got roots or not? Is it well centred, or is it sloping towards the right or left?

The treetop: is it contracted, stunted or too weak? Or is it in full bloom, stretching up and outwards, expressing the expansiveness of the personality of the drawer?

Branches

How many branches are there? Is the number of branches symbolically meaningful?

Branches split or forked; does the number of branches correspond to the age of the person or a time of rupture, or significant events? We look for points of rupture in the tree which recall times of difficulty, loss of someone close, separations and divorces, traumatic events.

Roots

The roots are the basis of the tree of life; they may indicate where an initial trauma lies, e.g., birth trauma or post-natal complications. They represent the sense of security and healthy contact with the earth, life and the unconscious.

Nests, Holes

Nests or holes in the tree trunk may symbolise times of halted development, or significant events, which may have occurred on inner or outer planes; times of illness, ruptures in the process of development due to major moves, divorce of parents, or perhaps the birth of another child in the family.

Fruits

Fruits should be counted to see if they correspond to the years of the person's life. Numbers which repeat themselves may represent ages when changes or traumatic events were recorded.

Seasons

Seasons are important; a Christmas tree in June, as symbol of the zenith, may represent a symbolic turning point in development.

Colours

Is the tree colourful or is it drawn in black pencil? If it's drawn in black pencil, there may be a defence against exposing oneself. It may also symbolise depression and lack of energy for life or a defence against emotions.

Shadows

What lurks in the shadow? What is on the edge of consciousness pushing to become conscious?

Notes

1 Jaffé and Jung, *Memories*, p. 67.
2 Jung, *CW* Vol. 13, p. 253, para. 304.
3 Ibid. p. 272, para. 350.
4 Ibid. p. 253 para. 304.
5 Ibid. p. 272, para. 350.

Chapter Twelve

The house drawing

As symbol the house is feminine and therefore a place of intimacy, nurturing, protection and containment.

The house is a reflection of one's life at home, the sense of security in the family, and how "home" is interpreted by the psyche of the person. Every house drawing is unique. What does the house convey? What is the feeling tone of the drawing? Is it a happy house, or a sad, static, empty house?

The house may represent the self, the roof the head, the floor the feet, the facade the persona; the access may be introverted or extraverted. The house may have many layers and many facets; the doors and windows may be open or closed.

Perhaps the facade, symbolising the persona, may point to the mask or attitude one holds before the world and society. Is there any connection to the outside world, or is the house isolated, barricaded or dull in colour? According to Jung, "*The house recurs very often as a symbol in dreams, and it generally means the habitual or inherited attitude, the habitual way of living, or something acquired, or perhaps the way one lives with the whole family.*"[1]

He also speaks of the house:

Everything is alive and our upper storey, consciousness, is continually influenced by its living and active foundations. Like the building it is sustained and supported by them. And just as the building rises freely out of the earth, so our consciousness stands as if above the earth in space with a wide prospect before it. But the deeper we descend into the house the narrower the horizon becomes, and the more we find ourselves in the darkness, till

finally we reach the naked bed-rock, and with it that prehistoric time when reindeer hunt-
ers fought for a bare and wretched existence against the elemental forces of wild nature.[2]

The following drawing is the house of a 20-year-old student who finds life at home oppressive and boring. As an introvert he finds it difficult to express what he feels; his house is static and closed. He yearns to be independent so as to follow his career and his own calling.

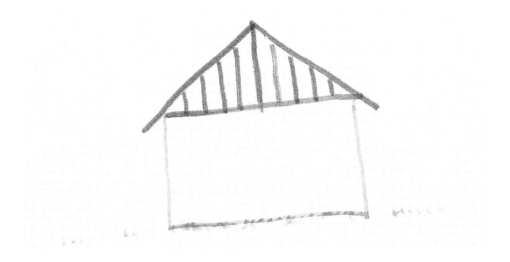

On the facing page, an extraverted 69-year-old grandmother lives with an open door. Family, friends and grandchildren are always welcome. Her house is a place of sunshine, warmth and happiness.

The drawing of a 16-year-old in a family of five who feels apart, isolated and lonely.

The following is a drawing of an eight-year-old child who lived in a family of four. This was a happy house full of light and sunshine for this child until one day Daddy left home and a light went out.

The window where the light went out suggests the integration of the situation and the psychic image of the event. She is in the process of transcending the trauma and the inner light that she experienced since her beginnings in the family is still lit. (Jody is an adopted child who is well-adjusted and confident).

In dreams there are often many rooms in the house, different floors, secret or unvisited rooms, forgotten rooms, or parts of the house that one has never known before. The house represents the psychic space; unknown rooms pertain to as yet undiscovered potential. The house on the very personal level may represent the life story of the person.

Annie now at 62 years old, realised after drawing her house that she had in fact drawn the stages of her life. At 40 she had found a meaningful relationship and then at 52 her partner died leaving her with a light which had also gone out on the fifth floor. Annie remains grateful for the time they had together and the work they had begun which still continues to shine a bright beam in her existence today. The tower for her represents the continuity of an ongoing creative process throughout the years of her life since she was 40 years old.

This is the house of a five-year-old with its five windows.

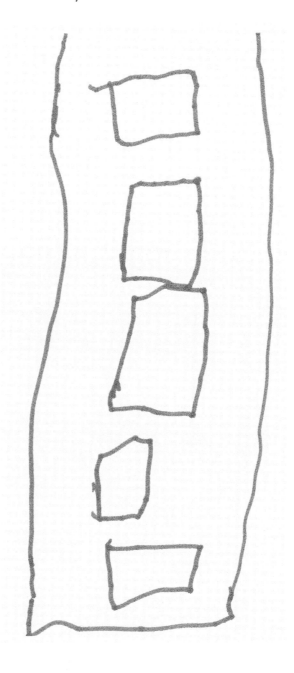

A house with no floor for this 14-year-old represents a lack of base, rootlessness and lack of security within the family and within himself. He has in fact moved house and country many times and his parents have a difficult relationship. There are four members in the family and he shares the upper floors with his twin brother.

Twelve-year-old Arty draws his house more open on the left-hand side towards the unconscious. The right side, facing towards the outer world and progressive development, seems blocked and closed off. Despite the introverted attitude of this drawing the chimney is letting out smoke suggesting thoughts and emotions. Can Arty find the means to express his feelings and emotions?

This is the house of a nine-year-old boy where the front walls are like a barricade, hindering any access. One might wonder what is happening inside. With the closed door and no windows one doesn't feel invited in; there is a defensive attitude, keeping others out. Are there family secrets that cannot be unveiled? Or does this point to a fear of invasion, of exposing any intimacy?

At the same time the roof is cut off pointing to a standstill in the psychological development of this young boy. What is the cause? Why has growth and progression been cut off? Has there been a specific trauma, separation or the death of someone in the environment?

In this case a 32-year-old man who is severely depressed feels he is up against a rock and claims he lacks access to life and others. He feels blocked in his depression and cannot open the door on his own.

Mary is seven years old at the time of drawing this house. It is clear that it is closed to the world and furthermore, as there are seven panels representing her seven years, it has likely been closed since the beginning. There are family secrets here too, and as the child is faithful, even to the unspoken codes, she will not let anyone discover what goes on behind closed walls. Mary lives in a small African village where the members of her family suffer from AIDS, but as this carries a stigma in her local environment the secret must not be exposed.

Johnny at six years old lives in two different houses as his parents are separated, but one house is more important than the other.

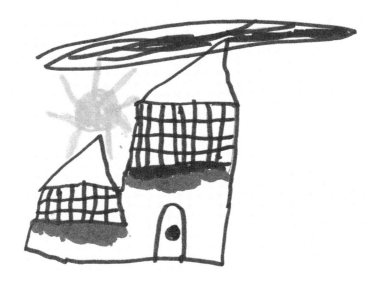

Betty at the same age lives a similar situation.

According to Chevalier and Gheerbrandt the house with its different levels is recognised in psychoanalysis as representing different levels of the psyche. "*The exterior of the house is the masque or the appearance of the person; the roof the head and the spirit, the centre of control of consciousness; the lower levels mark the level of the unconscious and instincts, the kitchen symbolizes the place of alchemical transformation or psychological transformations, which means a time of inner evolution.*"[3]

The soul window

Gerard Dorn, the medieval alchemist, spoke of the window of the soul as the "spiraculum," the breathing hole, or window on eternity. It is a place where the soul enters the body and eventually leaves it. In South America there is a custom of hitting the person just deceased hard on the head so as to open the hole at the top and free the soul. We find the same belief in African and other cultures.

It is curious to note that we often find this motif of the hole at the top of the house in spontaneous drawings and in all ages. Is it symbolic of an archetypal imprint from the ancient past, a remnant in the unconscious which lives on despite there being no recognition in any Western belief system of this concept?

Checklist for the house drawing

The house

Compare how big, open, closed or small the house is to the personality of the person drawing. Is the house well planted on its base, giving a sense of security and ground-edness, or does it lack a solid foundation?

Door

Is there a door, or no door? How big is the door compared to the house, and is it open or closed? Is it inviting in or blocking out any intrusion? Can one see inside, or not at all?

Windows

The transparent barriers of insight and protection represent the connection between the inner and outer worlds. Do they look out towards sunlight or into darkness? Are they big, allowing exposure, or small and defensive, or missing, not allowing anything on the inner plane to be revealed? Does the number of windows correspond to the number of persons living in the family? The window links the seen and the unseen, the concrete and the suspected, the inner and outer.

The roof

What is the roof like? Is it solid or rickety? Does it provide enough protection? "The roof may symbolise the mental level; is it too heavy, or overloaded? Or too light, insecure? Is it cut in half, unfinished, is the top missing? The cut-off roof would suggest that a process that has been cut off, interrupted by trauma or incapacity to adapt to a situation. Are there two roofs, as when parents are separated and the child lives in two different houses?

The chimney

Is there a chimney, showing a desire for expression? Is it letting out smoke, which would indicate emotions, anger or repressed feelings?

The path

Is there a path inviting others to enter, or that leads away from the house?

Stairs

Stairs lead the way up or down. They go towards consciousness and the world or descend into the unconscious and the lower realms. Many temples, cathedrals and holy sites have a symbolic number of stairs leading up or down representing the psychological and spiritual transition one must go through in approaching the sacred. Descending may lead to the other world where one meets the realm of dreams.

Gates and barriers

Gates and barriers define the limits of approach between the inner and outer worlds. Closed gates are symbols of protection which keep the unknown out. Gates are also markers of transition, as there is one sphere outside the gate, and another inside. In religious symbols, as in Buddhist stupas and Japanese toriis, the gate is a place of passage and initiation. In Eastern temples the gates protect from the profane and hold the sacred within. In Europe gates were sacred places and sacrifice was offered at the gates of cities to protect and sanctify the inner space. Open gates are welcoming and invite the outside in. Closed gates are private, defensive and protective.

Flowers and nature

Are there any decorations? Are there flowers and trees, which would represent dynamic nature and life?

Animals

Is there an animal, such as a cat or dog at the door, which suggest emotional attachments?

Missing elements

Is there anything superfluous or missing, such as no door or window?

Colours

What colour is the house? Grey? Red?

Orientation

Is the house leaning to the right or the left? Or, is it facing either way? Is the drawing of the house static or dynamic?

Notes

1 Jung, C.G. *Dream Analysis Notes on the seminars 1928–1930*, edited by William Mc
   Guire, Bollingen series XCIX, Princeton University Press, 1984.
2 Jung, *CW* Vol. 10, p. 32.
3 Chevalier et Ghebrandt, *Dictionnaire des Symbols*, Editions Robert Laffont, 1982.

Chapter Thirteen

The person drawing

The drawing of "the person" corresponds to two aspects: (1) the normal neurological integration that corresponds to body image, and (2) the psychological aspect which concerns the development of the sense of self, the narcissism of the personality, and the state of the ego.

With the development of ego consciousness comes an increased sensation of the sense of self. Jung in his late years remembered an event when as a child he "happened" to himself:

> I was taking the long road to school from Klein-Hüningen where we lived, to Basel, when suddenly for a single moment I had the overwhelming impression of having just emerged from a dense cloud. I knew, all at once: now I am myself! It was as if a wall of mist were at my back, and behind that wall there was not yet an "I" but at this moment I came upon myself. Previously I had existed too, but everything had merely happened to me. Now I happened to myself. Now I knew I am myself now, I exist. Previously I had been willed to do this and that. Now "I" willed. This experience seemed to me tremendously important and new: there was "authority" in me.[1]

The drawing of a child who has problems with neurological integration.

As does this child of 10 years old.

The "person drawing" includes the basic attitudes to life, introversion and extraversion and reflects the means to express oneself and to communicate. It illustrates the standpoint of the self in the world and in relation to others.

Buddy at five years old is an extravert like his father!

The parts of the body are symbolic and pertain to different psychological functions.

Hands relate to the means of contacting others and of manipulating the world. They have to do with communication and self-expressions. Hands indicate the nature of the relationship between inner and outer, between self and environment. Outstretched hands are contacting the world, the other. Missing hands show a sense of powerlessness and a lack of means to communicate with the environment. They suggest an inability to "handle" the world.

Head and hair have to do with the mental level, with thoughts and ideas. Too much hair would point to too much focus on the mental level, and perhaps even obsessional thoughts.

At 16 years old, Maddy has been diagnosed with bi-polar disorder. She complains that there is too much in her head. Her missing hands show that she consciously feels that she lacks the means to curb her impulses, and her sense of powerlessness makes her feel depressed and hopeless. She suffers from obsessional thoughts, and is constantly trying to understand what brought on her condition.

Everyone in the family has hands except the youngest, who at 14 years old still feels she hasn't quite found a place in her family.

Feet and legs have to do with the ego's standpoint, how one positions oneself in the environment and how one is anchored in life. No feet mean a loss of standpoint, loss of ground, insecurity, lack of earth element.

Mary and Margie have no feet, illustrating a lack of ego standpoint and a sensation of being poorly grounded in the collective.

The face has to do with narcissism and expression of self, with self-worth, confidence and self-appreciation. A red face expresses shame, embarrassment and the difficulty to feel at ease with oneself.

This is the drawing of a 12-year-old who has a physical problem of which she is ashamed and which makes her feel very self-conscious.

Her younger sister at five years old does not have any disability but she too feels embarrassment and a lacks a sense of self-worth and confidence.

Paul at 56 years old feels ill at ease with people and lacks any sense of self-appreciation or self-esteem.

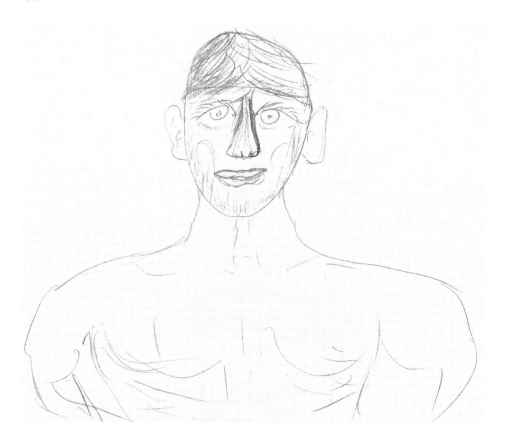

Despite a successful academic career, this student at 20 years old has a lack of self-esteem and feels he does not have the means to take his place in the world.

Moby at 18 years old feels depressed and lost and says he believes he has always felt that way for as long as he can remember. Moby's drawing shows an obviously depleted sense of self. The empty eyes express his feelings of being lost but also his incapacity to see where a path lies to help him advance in life.

Fran only has an upper body which may pertain to lack of attention to self, or to a fear of intimacy.

Turning one's back to the world expresses avoidance of exposure. There is a need to hide one's lack of assurance and sense of inadequacy.

June here communicates a healthy sense of self!

Checklist for person-drawing

Spatial orientation

What space and part of the sheet of paper does the person occupy? Is the figure mostly on the right or the left side of the page, or in the centre?

Colours

Is the figure colourful or pale, or drawn only in pencil?

Is the face red, pale or completely coloured? This represents the narcissism of the person. A coloured face may point to feelings of shame, rejection and inferiority.

Proportions

Is the head proportionate to the body? Is it too big, or too small? Is there too much hair? No hair?

Missing parts

What is missing?

Are the nose, ears and mouth drawn? The nose represents intuition, instinct and direction. The mouth is the means of verbal expression, the right to speak up and be heard as well as the ability to do so. The ears are for listening; no ears may indicate there are certain themes which the subject doesn't want to hear.

Are there hands? Are they open or closed? Do they give the impression of contacting the world or not?

Do the legs have feet? Is there any relationship to others in the drawing?

Expression

What is the facial expression? Is it sad, happy, rigid, fixed, open, smiling? Is the figure dynamic or reserved, introverted or extraverted?

Eyes

What does one notice about the eyes? Are the eyes wide open, or closed, or is one covered? Covered or closed eyes may pertain to a denial of a situation or defence against too much consciousness. Denial, which is to say not knowing about certain situations, may help to deal with what is going on in the environment.

Note

1   Jaffé and Jung, *Memories*, p. 32.

What to observe in a drawing

Developing the art of analysing drawings includes being receptive to what Jung called the "feeling tone" of the drawing, which means considering the atmosphere of the drawing and the effect it has upon us.

How is the drawing positioned on the page?

Horizontal lines tend to tell a story, whereas vertical lines make a statement.

In which direction does the drawing tend?

It is to the right or left of the page, indicating progression or regression of psychic energy?

Where do the barriers lie?

What is blocking the movement of libido?

What is central?

What motifs or symbols are repeated? Size of the motifs

What motifs are bigger and given more importance?

What is smaller, discreet, and tending towards consciousness? What is incoherent, superfluous or bizarre?

Is there a frame?

A looking from the inside out or from the outside in?

What colours are used?

Is there a lack of colour? What is drawn in pencil? Is there a tendency to avoid colour, which may show resistance, timidity, or a defence against emotions?

What numbers does one find?

For example, how many apples are on the tree, flowers in the meadow, etc.?

What is the relationship to the environment? What is missing?

What is emphasised, outlined in black or underlined? What are the written words?

Where do the shadows lie?

Are there attempts to erase?

This may show a need to correct, indicating auto-criticism or a lack of self-assurance.

Conclusion

One of the joys of spontaneous drawing lies in its limitlessness. Jung says; *"Where the safeguards afforded by specific aims fall away, unlimited possibilities emerge."*[1]

Every drawing is personal, unique and authentic. The fact that the technique applies regardless of race, culture, creed, sex or age, adds to its value as a means of communicating, expressing, investigating and developing.

When proposing spontaneous drawing it is important to allow whatever wants to express itself to emerge without preconceived intentions or ideas. A session is intended to provide a secure space for anything that the unconscious of the person wishes to produce, without prejudice or control.

First there is expression; then there is interpretation. Or, perhaps, no interpretation will be necessary. Expression itself may well be sufficient for the unconscious to recycle a theme without any interference on the part of the ego of the person drawing, or the analyst. Often just holding the space for the unconscious allows it to activate images and progress through its own autonomous process.

After many years of analysing and teaching, I find that the great majority of people of all ages and from many walks of life are willing and receptive to this approach. Spontaneous drawing relieves tension and reassures the person drawing, as there is always an instinctive aptitude which is mobilised; everyone knows how to draw a tree, a person or a house.

One must, however, remain humble before the unconscious, which knows so much more than the ego, and which often surprises with the material it produces arising out of complexes or traumas that are long forgotten and buried in its depths. Time does not change or influence trauma, but a conscious filtering of past events through a more mature ego can have a tremendously healing effect. One must always keep in mind that the unconscious has its own intention about the person's process and will provide all that is necessary for a healthy development to the next stage of maturity.

Self-realisation refers to a process of maturation, and this is the aim of the psyche itself: to develop the personality to its ultimate capacity, until wholeness is attained. To this end, spontaneous drawing has its place in any quest for self-development.

I conclude with Jung's own tribute to his almost forgotten soul:

> *This life is the way, the long sought after way to the unfathomable, which we call divine. There is no other way, all other ways are false paths: I found the right way, it led me to you, to my soul. I return tempered and purified. Do you still know me? How long the separation lasted! Everything has become so different. And how did I find you? How strange my journey was! What words should I use to tell you on what twisted paths a good star has guided me to you? Give me your hand, my almost forgotten soul. How warm the joy at seeing you again, you long disavowed soul. Life has led me back to you. Let us thank the life I have lived for all the happy and all the sad hours, for every joy, for every sadness. My soul, my journey should continue with you. I will wander with you and ascend to my solitude.[2]*

Notes
1   Jung, *CW* Vol. 8, p. 198.
2   Jung, *Liber Novus*, p. 232.

Index

Note: Page numbers in *italic* indicate figures on the corresponding pages.

Action Painting 2
adaptation 43–45, 50
ageing 50
alchemy 11, 69
Alfonso 89–99
Alice 137–138
amplification 80
Amy *81*, 81–86, *82*
analyses 157–160, 177–180, 181–182
analysts 80–81
animals 101–108, *103*, *104*, *105*, *107*, 159
Annie 148–149
archetypes 75, 77
Archive of Images 2
art 2
Art Brut 2
artists 1
"atman" 10
attachments 95
attitudes 15, 16, *16*, *17*, 50
auto-regulation 21–22

Bach, Susan 2–3
barriers 31, 159, 181
bears 91, *91*
bees 94

Betty 155
"big dreams" 78
Bildarchiv *see* Archive of Images
Billy 133
birds 64, *64*, 139, *140*
blockages 50–51, *51*, *56*
Bobby 109–127
branches 29, *29*, 141; broken 27, *27*, *28*

castration 99
cats 89
cave paintings 106, *107*
central positions 19, *19*
centring 23, *23*
children 1, 2–3, 51, 80–81
chimneys *152*, *157*, 158
coherence 20–21, *21*
collective unconscious 8, *14*, 18, 75–78,
    P–1
colours 142, 159, 178, 181
commitment 32
complexes 19
confidence 32
confusion *117*, *P–18*
conscious *14*, 41
crying 57, *57*

depression 23, 55
development 33, *33*, 46, *46*, 79, *P–2*
Dilly 130–132
directions 22, *22*, 181
dispersion 34, *35*
divisions 25, *25*
doors 158
Dubuffet, Jean 2

eggs 92
ego 13, *14*, *19*, 34, 41, *41*, *P–1*
equivalence 97
explosions 124, *124*
expressions 178
extraversion *14*, 16, *16*
eyes 179

facades 145
faces 169
fairy tales 49, 78, 105
families 30, *30*, *103*, *104*, *105*, 107; *see also* fathers; mothers; parents
fathers *39*, 40
feelings *14*, 15, *P–1*
"feeling tone" 16, 127, 136, 145, 181
feet 167–168
Firth, Gregg 3
fish *113*, *119*, *P–14*, *P–20*, *P–21*, *P–22*
flowers 159
focuses 20, *20*
foxes 92
fragmentation 36, *36*, *37*
framing *30*, 181
Freud, Sigmund 7, 43
friends *38*
fruits 142
functions 15, 21–22

gates 159
Green Man 62, *62*
growth 130; *see also* development

hair 165
hands 165–166
heads 165
healing 23
hearts *120*, 120–122, *121*, *122*
heroes 77, 97
holes 27, 141
honey 91, *91*
horizons *123*, *124*, *P–23*, *P–24*
houses *31*; analysis of 157–160; blocked *154*; closed *153*; and extroversion *147*; and floors *151*; and introversion *146*, *152*; and isolation *147*; levels of 156; and life stages *149*; separate *155*; as symbols 145–157; and trauma *148*; and windows *151*

identification 38, *38*, *39*, 39–40
images 10–11, 33, *33*
incoherence 20–21, *21*
inferior functions *14*, *P–1*
instincts 75, 77
interpretations 183
intimacy 175
introversion *14*, *16*
intuition *14*, 15, *P–1*

Jacky 132
Janie *56*; and blockages 55–57, 63, *63*; and freedom *P–8*, *P–9*; inner world of 60–62, *61*, *62*, *P–6*, *P–7*; and suffering 57, 57–59, *58*, *59*, *P–3*, *P–4*, *P–5*
jewels *85*, *86*
Johnny 155
Jonah 48, *48*
Jung, Carl *76*; on art 4; on attitudes 50; on collective unconscious 75; on development 67; on the ego 34; on growth 47; on his soul 184; on houses 145–146; on instincts 77; on libido 43, 95; life of 7–12; on mandalas 93; on the

psyche 13; on self 161; on
  suggestions 99; on symbols 69, 73;
  on transcendent function 79–80;
  on trees 129
Jung, Emma 9

keys *81, 82*
knots 27, *27*

labyrinths 89, *90*, 96
legs 167–168
levels 156
Liber Novus see Red Book
libido 14, 43, 49, *49*, 50; *see also* progression;
  regression
lines 181
lions *102*
loneliness *56*
lower spheres 23, *23, 52*

Maddy 165–166
mandalas 9–10, 92
Mary 154
masses *P–15, P–16, P–17*
mental illness 2, 7
mice 96, *96*
Mike 138
missing elements 159, 178
Moby 174
monsters *82, 83, 84*, 86
mothers *39*
motifs 18, 30, *30*, 70, 181
movement 22, *22*
mythological themes 18
myths 47, *47*, 75, 78, 105

nature 159
nests 92, *93*, 141
neurological integration *162, 163*
night sea journeys 48–49
numbers *23, 23*–24, 181

off the page 32, *32*
orientation 159, 177
outsiders 2
owls 72, *72*, 96, *96*, 99

parents 139; see also families; fathers;
  mothers
paths 158
people *P–13*; analysis of 177–180; and
  extraversion *164*; and eyes *179, 180*; and
  feet *168*; and hands *165, 166, 167*; and
  self-esteem *169, 170, 171, 172, 173, 174,
  175, 176, 177*; as symbols 161–177
personalities 15
"personality number 2" 7
personal themes 18
personal unconscious *14*, 18, *P–1*
progression 43–45, *44, 46, 53, P–2*
proportions 178
psyches 8, 13, 78
psychiatry 7–8
psychoid 13
psychoid spheres *14, P–1*

Rainmaker 49
Red Book, The 9, 76, *P–11*
regression 43–45, *44, 45, 46, 52*, 55, *P–2*
repetitions 23, 25
representation collectives 48
repression 34
roofs 153, 158
roots 135–136, 141
ruins 97

San people 49
seasons 142
self 161
self-esteem 170–174
self-realisation *46*, 184, *P–2*
sensations *14*, 15, *P–1*
sexual drive 43

shadow, the *14, P–1*
shadows 142, 182
shamans 101
signs 70
skull-and-cross-bones *118, P–19*
souls 11, 184
splitting 25, *25*, 34
spontaneous drawings 3–4, 183–184;
    definition of 1; and the ego 34; and
    libido 45; and symbols 73; and the
    unconscious 2
stairs 158–159
Starsky, David *98*, 98–99
structures 14
submarines *92*
suggestions 99
superior functions *14*
swords *83, 84*, 86
symbols 69–73, *71, 72*, 79, 106
Symbols of Transformation 8

themes 18
Theseus 47, *47*, 96–97
thinking 15, *P–1*

toads 94, *94*
Tommy 135–136
totemism 101–108
transcendent function 79–87
transformation 48
trees *32, 33, 110, 125, 126, 130, 131,
    132*, 133, *143, P–12, P–25*; analysis
    of 141–142; and branches *28, 29*;
    and growth 131–134; and knots *27*;
    and mourning *139*; and roots *135*,
    135–136, *136*; and self 125–127; and
    splitting *24, 26, 137*, 138; as symbols
    129–130, 141
treetops 141

unconscious 2, 13, 15, *P–2*; *see also*
    collective unconscious; personal
    unconscious
upper spheres *22*, 22–23

volcanoes 97

windows 156, 158
Wolff, Toni 9